THE FIVE WOUNDS

*Dedicated to Alison Davis
who has offered up so much suffering
for this work*

THE FIVE WOUNDS

SANCTUARY FOR THE SICK
BALM FOR THE WOUNDED
SPIRIT

ANN FARMER

GRACEWING

First published in England in 2012
by
Gracewing
2 Southern Avenue
Leominster
Herefordshire HR6 0QF
United Kingdom
www.gracewing.co.uk

No part of this publication may be reproduced, stored in a retrieval system, or transmitted in any form or by any means, electronic, mechanical, photocopying, recording or otherwise, without the written permission of the publisher.

The right of Ann Farmer to be identified as the author of this work has been asserted in accordance with the Copyright, Designs and Patents Act 1988.

© 2012 Ann Farmer

ISBN 978 085244 781 9

Typeset by Gracewing

On the cover: detail from Hans Memling, *The Man of Sorrows in the Arms of the Virgin* (1475).

CONTENTS

Preface..vii

Introduction..1

Chapter One: Betrayed...33

Chapter Two: Who Am I?...39

Chapter Three: Why Me?...45

Chapter Four: Humiliated..57

Chapter Five: Forsaken..67

Conclusion: Balm for a Wounded Spirit....................73

Addendum: A Note on Suicide..................................79

Bibliography...87

Useful organizations...94

Prayers and devotions...95

Preface

For most of my life I have been interested in politics, and for almost all my adult life I have been pro-life. Anyone involved in the pro-life movement will know that politics is inseparable from it; indeed, politics is involved in everything, including sickness and disability. With two disabled brothers, and a brother-in-law (RIP) who faced quadriplegia with courage, fortitude and good humour, I was already against eugenics and euthanasia; however, nothing concentrates the mind quite so much as personal experience. In 2002 I began to suffer from muscle weakness and extreme exhaustion, as well as digestive problems that made eating and drinking difficult. With my mobility severely restricted, I have experienced the isolation of sickness—but in that isolation, a greater closeness to God. I wanted to share the resulting spiritual insights with other sufferers, and that is how *The Five Wounds* began. The first draft of the manuscript was completed in 2007, but clearly God had more to teach me about the mystery of suffering.

In studying the healing miracles of Jesus it quickly became evident that there is a difference of experience between those who are born with a condition, and those who acquire a disability or disabling disease along the way. Those who are born into disability can face problems of discrimination, injustice and sometimes bullying from the very beginning, and I especially thank Alison Davis for her perspective on this problem. People who become disabled face some of the same issues, but also a kind of bereavement as we mourn the loss of abilities we often took for granted, along with friendships, occupations and pastimes. However, all of us face negative views of disability, which now threaten our very right to life: under the rhetoric of 'choice' a vigorous campaign is being fought for the 'right' to die. Throughout history, people have fought for the right to live—to be spared from death—but now it is claimed that disabled and sick people need to be spared from life. Some of the campaign's prominent spokespeople are disabled; they promote the message that being cared for is undignified and that suicide or being killed equals a dignified death, a view encapsulated in the Voluntary Euthanasia Society's change of name to Dignity in Dying. However, most disabled people want to be cared for; we do not want to kill ourselves, or be killed by anyone else. Nonetheless, the daily struggle to stay alive is sometimes exhausting, spiritually as well as physically and mentally; sometimes will power is not enough, and then the siren voices promising a timed exit can be seductive.

Against this background of soothing slogans, I wish to pose some deeper questions: is life simply about doing what we want, when we want? Or is there more to life than just 'doing'? Is 'being' not enough? However, should we always value quantity of life over quality? Is there any point to life when it involves suffering, and are laws against helping someone commit suicide unnecessarily restrictive—an insult in an age of personal autonomy? Is it compassionate to keep someone alive, or is it more compassionate to end suffering by ending life - or is this view merely a mask for callousness, with compassion directed not to the sufferer, but to those who would rather 'pass by on the other side'? (Lk 10:31–32) While such questions may be of academic interest to the 'chattering classes',[1] they are literally a matter of life or death to those whose lives depends on others. We hear much about the 'glass ceiling' that prevents people from reaching their full potential in life, but experience has taught me that sickness and disability place us on the other side of a glass window through which we can see and be seen by the able-bodied, who, however, see only the suffering. They cannot reach us without a conscious effort at empathy; consequently, they are vulnerable to the argument that if disabled people are suffering they must want to kill themselves. In reality, people adjust to disability and sickness—it is the depressed that tend to kill themselves.

The euthanasia and assisted suicide movement argues that disabled people kill themselves not out of depression but as a rational choice; but no one has ever killed themselves out of happiness. Campaigners claim they are not targeting disabled people, but in urging people to sign 'living wills'—irrevocable and legally binding documents stating that they do not wish to be treated should they fall sick or become disabled - they are encouraging people to avoid disability by giving some unknown person permission to kill them in unknown circumstances at some time in the unknowable future; in effect, 'living wills' would deny people the choice to change their minds and adapt to a new situation. Rather than giving people more choice, death means the end of all choices. The unavoidable implication of the 'right to die' campaign is that disabled and sick people would be better off dead; moreover, rationally, it should apply to everyone when they begin to acquire the disabilities of old age. Even if the 'artist's impression' of a future without suffering still appeals to those who have forgotten the lessons of history, or are unaware of the brutal reality of Hitler's murderous campaign against the sick and disabled,[2] their campaign impacts negatively on sick and disabled people: instead of discussing possible cures and improvements in care, the public mind is focussed on the expense of prolonging 'useless' lives, at the expense of their own health needs. Those who are fighting for the right to live and to be cared for, and against the fear of becoming a burden on others, find the continual focus on death most depressing; by focussing instead on the Wounds of Christ and how they can help those who suffer, this work will help those struggling to swim against the tide of death, giving them hope and help to carry on living; most of all, it will bring them closer to God, source of all life, who is with us in the fight for life.

My thanks go to Alison Davis for her help in the writing of *The Five Wounds*, and to Gracewing, especially to Father Paul Haffner, for his help in getting the work into print; also to the nuns who taught me, long before I realised the implications, about the dangers of presumption and despair.

Notes

[1] Dr Peter Saunders, director of the anti-euthanasia charity *Care Not Killing*, accused the BBC of being a 'cheerleader for assisted suicide' after broadcasting a film showing a man being helped to commit suicide at the Dignitas centre in Switzerland (*Daily Mail*, 15 April 2011).

[2] See: M. Burleigh, *Death and Deliverance: 'Euthanasia' in Germany 1900-1945* (Cambridge: Cambridge University Press, 1994).

Introduction

Why the Five Wounds?

Christians are familiar with the Wounds of Christ: His hands and feet bore the imprint of the nails that fastened Him to the cross, and His side, the mark of the soldier's spear (Jn 19:32–35). Perhaps we are too familiar with them, for the impact of His wounds, sustained for our sake, has resonated throughout history: they have been seen as a deep consolation but also a potent threat. The medieval devotion to the Five Wounds depicted the hands, feet and side of Christ surrounded by the implements of the Passion—the lance, spear, scourges, nails, and crown of thorns, itself connected to the devotion to the Sacred Head of Jesus.[1] In *The Stripping of the Altars* Eamon Duffy describes prayers, poems and Masses dedicated to the image. Popes offered generous indulgences—'time off' from Purgatory—for those who prayed before the Five Wounds. Wealthy people could contemplate it, beautifully illustrated, in their lavishly decorated prayer books; the poor displayed cheap prints of the Five Wounds in their homes.

The devotion originated in the Church of Santa Croce in Rome, which housed an early medieval Byzantine icon depicting the implements of the Passion; the church had a chapel to Pope St Gregory, with whom the devotion became associated, and from there it spread across Europe, becoming a popular focus for pilgrims.

The influence of the Five Wounds of Jesus can be seen throughout Christendom, spanning East and West; indeed, it is encapsulated in the five crosses of the red Jerusalem Cross, the 'Crusaders' Cross'. In many Christian churches, when the altar is consecrated, it is anointed in five places to indicate the Five Holy Wounds. Some Eastern Orthodox churches have five domes to symbolise the Five Holy Wounds—an alternative symbolism to that of Christ and the Four Evangelists. In the twelfth and thirteenth centuries, St Bernard of Clairvaux and St Francis of Assisi encouraged devotions and practices in honour of the Five Wounds of the Passion. Some of the prayers honouring the Wounds have been attributed to St Clare of Assisi and St Mechthild. The fourteenth century holy mystic St Gertrude of Helfta had a holy vision that Christ sustained 5,466 wounds during the Passion. St Bridget of Sweden popularised the recitation of fifteen Paternosters every day in remembrance of the Sacred Wounds. A special Mass of the Five Wounds was known as the Golden Mass, and in the fourteenth century the monastery of Fritzlar in Thuringia held the earliest known feast in honour of the Wounds of Christ, on the Friday after the octave of Corpus Christi. By the fifteenth century it had spread as far as Salisbury, Wiltshire, and to Huesca and Jaca in Spain; to Vienna and Tours. It was included in the Breviaries of many orders, including the Carmelites, Franciscans, and Dominicans. In Portugal the Festa das Cinco Chagas do Senhor (the Feast of the Five Wounds of the Lord) acquired historical and political significance: celebrated since the Middle Ages at Evora and elsewhere on 6th February (at Lisbon, on the Friday after Ash Wednesday) it commemorated the founding of the Portuguese kingdom. In 1139, before the Battle of Ourique, Christ appeared to Alfonso Henriquez, promising victory over the Moors and instructing him to include the emblem of the Five Wounds in the new Portuguese coat of arms. To this day the feast is celebrated in all Portuguese-speaking countries. In Venice, the 1766 Proper (that part of the liturgy specific to the date in the Liturgical Year) contains possibly the earliest series of movable feasts in honour of Christ's Passion; the Feast of the Five Wounds is on the second Sunday in March; in 1809 it was granted to Livorno for the Friday after Ash Wednesday, and is still kept on this day in many Tuscan dioceses, and elsewhere, for example in Mexico. In Rome, in 1831, the feasts in honour of the Passion were adopted by the Passionist order, the feast being assigned for the City to the Friday after the third Sunday in Lent.

However, the Five Wounds was not simply a colourful image: in England, in the York Miracle Play of the Judgement, Christ displayed His Wounds to the people, attended by angels bearing the Instruments of His Passion, and acted out the story of the sheep and the goats (Mt 25) in which He judges men on how they treat the needy and the sick. The Wounds were not merely to be looked at, but were a call to action. The devotion made a deep impression on the English, expressed in prayers and Masses but also acts of charity: the visionary Margery Kempe said she could not pass a leper or sick person without seeing the Wounds of Christ. As Eamon Duffy notes, by doing acts of charity, people 'could turn the Wounds of Judgement into Wounds of Mercy, forestalling the condemnation threatened in Matthew 25 by attending, while there was still time, to Christ's wounded members, the poor.' Such was the popularity of the devotion that even the Reformation could not entirely stamp it out — indeed, in 1536 the image was borne aloft by the Pilgrimage of Grace, the northern uprising, a symbol of rebellion against the abandonment of the Old Faith and the spiritual desolation of the new. Far from being solely 'a simple affective devotion to the Passion', the Five Wounds expressed the Catholic theology of Salvation: 'It is hardly surprising, therefore, that the symbol... should have been chosen by the Pilgrims of Grace as the emblem of their loyalty to the whole medieval Catholic system.'[2]

The Pilgrimage of Grace was the people's response to the suppression of the religious houses by Henry VIII; it emerged in 1536 in Lincolnshire, at Louth and Horncastle, where the banner of the Five Wounds first appeared. Elsewhere it was adopted as an emblem as the insurrection spread to Yorkshire, to Hull, and to Durham and Northumberland. The Pilgrims had 'a simple desire for the restoration of religion', singing as they marched:

Chryst crucifydd,
For they woundes wyde
Us Commons guyde,
Which pilgrims be...[3]

The Five Wounds was also adopted as the emblem of the Western Rising of 1549, a response to the replacement of the Latin Mass by the English Prayer Book. Despite ushering in an era of unprecedented religious strife and persecution, historically the Reformation has been presented as an advance for the English, empowering ordinary people by releasing them from the grip of Rome and superstition; but many in Cornwall did not speak English anyway,[4] and in the old Latin Mass the Our Father had been recited in Cornish. Thousands of Cornishmen besieged Exeter to demand a return to the old ways; they were only defeated by 'foreign mercenaries hired for the Scottish wars'.

Disturbances began in Devon when an old woman was 'molested for saying her rosary in public'; in Sampford Courtenay, parishioners 'persuaded their priest to continue to say Mass publicly in defiance of the law'. The insurgents demanded 'the sacrament hung over the high altar, and thus to be worshipped as it was wont to be', with 'holy bread and holy water every Sunday, palms and ashes at the time accustomed, images to be set up again in every church, and all other ancient ceremonies held heretofore by our Mother Holy Church.'[5] The 'massed commons', in their last peaceful attempt to take Exeter, marched '[b]ehind the banner of the Five Wounds', with 'priests in their chasubles, following the canopy under which was carried the Blessed Sacrament'.[6]

The unrest spread to Sussex, Surrey, Kent, Oxfordshire, Somerset, Wiltshire, and Hampshire;[7] at Winchester, a group of Catholic men ordered 'a banner to be made, similar to that of the Western rebels, depicting the Five Wounds, with the chalice and Host and a priest kneeling in adoration'.[8] Henry VIII, although he declared himself Supreme Head of the Church of England, continued to adhere to the Catholic religion, but under his son Edward VI a full-blooded Protestantism was unleashed.[9] It destroyed all images in churches, including the statues on rood ('cross') screens and stained glass windows. The burning of all lights in church, fast and feast days, the saying of the Rosary, and all pilgrimages and processions, were banned.[10] The suppression of the Western rebellion 'signalled the decline of religious devotion among the people of Devon and Cornwall, which was symbolised in the banner of the Five Wounds'.[11] Though the image of Christ's Wounds had been eradicated, it continued to haunt the popular imagination; it was rekindled in the eighteenth century with the arrival of John Wesley and Methodism, a brand of worship whose hymns reflected earlier religious imagery in emphasising the healing power of Christ's Blood, and the Wounds of Christ as a place of refuge:

> *O precious Side-hole's cavity*
> *I want to spend my life in thee. ...*
> *There in one Side-hole's joy divine,*
> *I'll spend all future Days of mine.*
> *Yes, yes, I will forever sit*
> *There, where thy Side was split.*[12]

Nonetheless, with the death of popular Catholic piety in England, a visible dimension of invisible faith was virtually eradicated. The Reformation had not introduced a new religion to a theologically illiterate peasantry—the people already believed—but proscribed the religious practices that expressed that belief: devotion to the Sacred Head, Hands and Feet of Jesus emerged from the startling realisation that

God actually possessed a head, hands and feet. Far from superstitious, Catholicism had tamed the bloody and ruthless superstitions of paganism: what God had created was good (Ex 1:31) but the creation must not be worshipped instead of the Creator (Ex 20:3).

Catholic piety endowed the natural world with Christian meaning, interweaving Christian theology with the love of Nature and popular myth: for example, the tiny colourful goldfinch was said to have attempted to 'pull a thorn, from the crown of thorns, from Jesus' forehead. In the process it was splashed with a drop of Jesus' blood, which became the permanent red mark on its head'.[13] It was Christ, not the bird that was worshipped; blood was not to be sacrificed, but Christ's Blood was sacred because by shedding it He had saved the world. In a rational progression, elements that were involved in this Salvation became objects of veneration, speaking to the heart in a language that even the humblest could understand, and the least humble could not ignore: in churches the Crown of Thorns, seen along with the other instruments of Christ's Passion, became a symbol of Good Friday;[14] the Sacred Heart of Jesus was often depicted in churches surrounded by thorns from the Crown.[15] Objects of pagan worship became infused with Christian meaning: the spines of the holly leaf came to 'represent the crown of thorns', with 'the red berries drops of blood, and the bitter bark the Passion', as recalled in the popular Christmas carol:

The holly and the ivy
When they are both full grown
Of all the trees that are in the wood
The holly tree bears the crown...[16]

Paradoxically, 'superstitious practices' like that of the Five Wounds and the Sacred Head of Jesus had brought the whole world, political as well as natural, under the reign of Christ the King instead of the temporal rule of capricious kings and unpredictable Mother Nature; evil no longer controlled the universe, but took its place under the rule of God—like the gargoyles, hapless evil spirits, perched high up on the cathedral roofs where they were made to spout dirty water under God's watchful messengers, the angels. Popular Catholic piety, following in the tradition begun by God at the Incarnation, had made truth visible; most importantly, it was to be held in common. Protestantism did not dispute this truth, but it disputed on the way we were to get to Heaven—by faith, not 'works'.

The tension between faith and works was nothing new, as St James pointed out: 'Someone will say, "You have faith and I have works." Show me your faith apart from your works, and I by my works will show you my faith' (Jm 2:18). Luther removed the Letter of St James from the Bible, calling it an 'epistle of straw' because it conflicted with his belief in justification by faith alone.[17] At the same time, visible reminders were removed from the sixteenth-century English theological landscape. Faith became a private matter as the English people went in fear of Sir Francis Walsingham's network of spies.[18] As future generations were deprived of visible reminders—even the sign of the Cross—faith would be confined to the hearts and minds of the people; even worse, they would be separated from Jesus in the Eucharist, and deprived of the help of the Communion of Saints. Religion, once expressed in all the colours of the rainbow, would become as black and white as the letters in the Bible in a whitewashed church, where even the worshippers would be clad in black and white. Like the abbeys, which did not decay into picturesque ruins through disuse, but were closed and systematically dismantled, Catholicism as a way of life did not die out but had to be broken up and stamped out.

As religion was driven into the private sphere, so was charity: the Reformation had 'privatised' the monastery lands and incomes of the chantries, where priests received stipends to pray for dead benefactors,[19] but the State did not take over the monks' role in caring for the poor and sick. The two factors were intimately connected, because as belief in Purgatory for rich and poor alike was abolished, and the 'doom' paintings in churches, depicting the Last Judgement, were whitewashed over, it was the poor rather than the rich who were made to feel as if it would be easier to go through the eye of a needle than to get into Heaven (Mt 19:23–24). Margery Kempe's compunction at passing a beggar and seeing in him the Wounds of Christ was replaced by the indifference of Dives, the 'rich man... clothed in purple and fine linen... who feasted sumptuously every day', to Lazarus (Lk 16:19–21).

Like the wall paintings depicting the spiritual equality of the Judgement, the sins of the wealthy could be more easily whitewashed; enriched by the despoliation of Church property, they enjoyed the beauty of art in their privacy of their homes, and bought comfortable pews in whitewashed churches while the poor stood at the back.[20] The suffering Christ was replaced by the triumphant Christ, and the poor lost the visual reminders that had comforted the afflicted but also afflicted the comfortable.[21]

The monks had been portrayed by Henry VIII's Commissioners of Enquiry as lazy and shiftless, but they had performed an important function in caring for the poor and the sick, as became apparent after the monasteries were dissolved. Henry passed harsh laws in response to the 'sturdy beggars' who had formerly been fed at the monastery gates as they tramped from town to town. In 1547, under Edward VI, vagrants were subjected to two years' servitude and branding with a 'V'; in 1601 Elizabeth I made poor relief the responsibility of the parish, and able-bodied beggars who refused to work could be beaten or placed in Houses of Correction. The poor and sick had become a 'problem' to be 'dealt with'.[22]

Time and again Christian compassion clashed with the utilitarian and pragmatic approach that saw suffering as useless—as a moral failing, even—the same approach that would have killed Jesus on the Cross to prevent His suffering. The Crucifix, as a reminder of the Old Ways, had been removed, and Margery Kempe's beggar was no longer a visible reminder to men of the Wounds of Christ—an uncomfortable reminder of their own mortality. Dives averted his eyes from Lazarus's sores lest it spoil his appetite for dinner; now, people were motivated to clear away poverty, sickness and disability because they formed a blight on an otherwise fair landscape. Christian charity began to be seen as exacerbating the problem, and even Christians were not immune to this belief: in the eighteenth century an Anglican parson, Thomas Malthus, saw the poor not as producers of wealth or even fellow human beings, but as hangers-on at the banquet of life whose numbers would increase until they literally starved to death; he urged that empty cottages be pulled down to prevent the poor proliferating; he also inspired the system of Workhouses, immortalised by Charles Dickens in *Oliver Twist*, where males and females were separated to prevent the poor from multiplying.[23]

Charles Darwin was indebted to Malthus for his work *On the Origin of Species* (1859) and the public mind, nurtured on a tale of religious evolution from primitive Catholicism to sophisticated Protestantism, was ripe to receive this new gospel explaining how sophisticated life forms evolved from more primitive organisms.[24] Apparently, there was no longer a Fall (Ex 3:1–24)[25] but the ever-present fear of the 'fall back' into the swamp from which Man had emerged: in *The Descent of Man* (1871) Darwin described how the human race could degenerate, warning that charity to the poor was responsible for this degeneration by encouraging the worst and sickliest elements to breed.[26] Herbert Spencer's 'the survival of the fittest' expressed a view of Victorian economics as an evolutionary process under which the weakest lost out.[27]

Darwin's cousin, Francis Galton, attempted to make a scientific religion of evolution, called 'eugenics', in which the healthy, wealthy and white were seen as superior—more 'evolved'—than those inferior, lesser evolved organisms, the sickly, poor and non-white.[28] Galton began a movement dedicated to encouraging 'better breeding', and discouraging the breeding of the less-than-perfect; it would advocate the prevention of 'misery' by preventing the birth of human beings by contraception, sterilisation and abortion; it would also urge the 'compassionate solution' of euthanasia for the sick—indeed, for many diseases, like tuberculosis, that are now curable.[29] Some eugenicists even discussed the 'lethal chamber' for 'hopeless cases' long before Hitler,[30] and when the Nazis, who idolised health and fitness, rose to power, English eugenicists praised his compulsory sterilisation of the 'unfit'.[31]

Catholic culture was and is far from perfect; all the men Jesus appointed as Disciples were weak men; but as Chesterton remarked of a famous 'strong man', Hitler, 'the strong man is he who can really face the fact that he is weak';[32] the Church has always recognised human weakness, as well as the value of constant reminders of this fact; thus, when the Reformation favoured the bare cross over the crucifix in order to emphasise the Resurrection, a powerful visual reminder of Christ's suffering, and of all human weakness and suffering, was lost to the Christian imagination. It became easier for those who did not wish to spoil a comfortable earthly life by contemplating the uncertainties of the afterlife, to address poverty with schemes based more on the need to tidy away the problem, as their ancestors had cleared away the crucifixes.

The Cross continued to challenge earthly interpretations of power into the twentieth century: the Nazis were only too aware of its power, and began a campaign of destruction against holy crosses in churches and in wayside shrines;[33] they also ordered the removal of crucifixes from German classrooms in a bid to erase Christian influence[34]—by no means the last such attempt in modern times, as shown by a lengthy legal battle in Italy.

This 'back-handed compliment' to the power of the Cross was reflected in attitudes to English Catholics after the Reformation; subjected to heavy financial penalties, they were not emancipated until 1829, and remained figures of suspicion—even paranoia, as the most famous English convert, Blessed John Henry Newman, noted,[35] suspected of constantly plotting to take over the country.[36]

Nonetheless, English non-Catholic Christianity produced some of the most inspirational, compassionate and humanitarian figures as well as the pragmatists—Florence Nightingale and Elizabeth Fry as well as Thomas Malthus and Francis Galton; the modern hospice movement as well as the euthanasia campaign.[37] The inspirational figures proposed practical solutions to sickness and need—but in the service of a higher justice and truth; they had the ability to galvanise the popular imagination through words and pictures in ways that resonated in the English soul. This crusading religion was in a large part literary: pre-eminent amongst its prophets and priests was William Shakespeare, who in Elizabethan times had promoted a Catholic viewpoint that trod the dangerous line between truth and treason: his plays warned of human failings, the pitfalls of power overcoming Christian kindness, and the perils of Purgatory—for Catholics as well as Protestants.[38]

Charles Dickens, with his hatred of hypocrisy and compassion for the downtrodden, the outcast, the sick and the disabled, depicted one of his heroes, Barnaby Rudge, as mentally disabled, long before the era of equality and diversity.[39] Dickens's miser Ebenezer Scrooge saved Christmas with a single word: 'Humbug!'[40] On being told that many poor people would rather die than enter the Workhouse, Scrooge remarked: 'If they would rather die… they had better do it, and decrease the surplus population';[41] however, Scrooge is converted to compassion by ghosts; as with Shakespeare, in Dickens' stories they continue to influence earthly life, and in *A Christmas Carol* he vividly portrays the afterlife in a terrifying scene where souls in a ghostly Purgatory lament their failure to help the poor and needy during their earthly lives.[42]

The English people continued to be influenced by the visual, in words as well as pictures; the wounds of the poor and sick may have been overlooked when the Wounds of Christ were forgotten, but poets continued to recall them to the public imagination. In the eighteenth century, while wealthy patrons of the arts commissioned portraits of their favourite animals, with perhaps some rosy-cheeked peasants driving sheep in the background, William Hogarth's cartoons satirised vice and folly, drawing attention to the connection between lust and cruelty, and the plight of its helpless victims, innocent children, for whom he helped establish the first Foundling Hospital in London.[43] The mystic William Blake kept alive the burning desire for justice with his poem *Jerusalem*, which pictured Jesus, 'the Holy lamb of God', coming to England, contrasting the Industrial Revolution's 'dark satanic mills' with a vision of a new Jerusalem built in 'England's green and pleasant land'.[44]

In response to the blackened ugliness of Victorian industrialism driven by the scientific and economic imperative, William Morris and the pre-Raphaelite painters reclaimed 'Medievalism', long a byword for backwardness, superstition and squalor, in a burst of colour and romanticism; in their art and craft they made truth visible, clearing away the lies of history as if cleaning the soot from a broken stained glass window. G. K. Chesterton called the Reformation 'the revolt of the rich';[45] much earlier, the radical Tory, Anglican William Cobbett, said it had been 'engendered in beastly lust', resulting in 'that misery, that beggary, that nakedness, that hunger, that everlasting wrangling and spite, which now stare us in the face and stun our ears at every turn'.[46] William Morris linked the 'Medieval revival' to issues of social justice; English socialists and trades unionists, inspired by the Medieval guilds, marched under the colourful banners of their trades and addressed each other as brother and sister, infused with the early Christian idea that all goods should be held in common, and that sickness and want should be addressed as a Christian duty (Ac 2:44).[47]

Such aspirations formed the basis for the modern Welfare State, with its National Health Service; however, with the rise of militant Atheism, a new 'Reformation' has attempted once again to stamp out the Cross, specifically as worn by nurses; even offering to say a prayer for a patient has been ruled out.[48] While 'assisted suicide' is promoted for those unable to kill themselves, elderly patients suffer dehydration and malnutrition because they are unable to feed their selves.[49] Under the influence of the Cross, the poor and vulnerable were regarded as objects of pity and care; under that same influence, it was arranged for the State to carry out that care; however, now, under the Welfare State, patients cannot insist on being treated, but can opt not to be treated.[50] The imperative to care has been replaced by the imperative to cure, but when there is no cure, the lack of care can prove deadly. At the Reformation, the monks' skill in herbs was lost, leading to a centuries-long medical hiatus in which knowledge had to be re-learned, a slow and often painful process for both doctors and patients; neither did the advent of modern medicine signal a problem-free era: over-reliance on powerful pharmaceutical drugs and antibiotics has led to unwelcome side-effects, and the rise of 'superbugs'.[51] Now, ironically, herbal remedies are under threat from new regulations that insist on expensive tests to prove their safety.[52] This brief historical excursion into the influence of the visual on the spiritual, and its ramifications for the poor and sick, shows that without constant reminders of Original Sin, but also of God's scheme of Salvation, Man is doomed to repeat past errors; that his enduring sickness is the sickness of the spirit, for which true salvation comes not from science or medicine, but from God, the source of all life — of eternal life.

Until people saw the Wounds of Christ they could not fully appreciate the price Christ paid for their salvation. History shows that unless people see depictions of injustice — as with slavery, the plight of industrial workers and slum-dwellers — it is too easy to ignore it. In the modern age, the television drama *Cathy Come Home* had a huge impact on the public imagination, raising consciousness about homelessness;[53] television reports on the Ethiopian famine of 1984 brought images of starvation into comfortable homes worldwide, and led to the birth of the fund-raising charity Live Aid.[54] In the case of abortion, publicity surrounding the advent of three-dimensional scans used to detect disabilities in the womb, led to renewed interest in the right to life of the unborn. In contrast, the secretive Courts of Protection set up under the Mental Capacity Act of 2005 to adjudicate on whether mentally disabled people should have abortions, be sterilised, or be allowed to starve and dehydrate to death, are conducted under a system that forbids reporting of all but the bare outlines of cases; those whose fate is under discussion are referred to only by letters of the alphabet.[55] Injustice will never be fully addressed until the public sees the victims of injustice. Christ, the innocent victim of injustice, invites us to study his physical wounds not as a purely intellectual exercise — not even solely as a private devotion — but as an exercise in justice that can heal our spiritual wounds, and those of the societies in which we live. The image of Christ's wounds is not an out-dated curiosity, therefore, but represents eternal truth captured in time, speaking afresh to new generations: the Truth that is Christ.

Contemplating Christ's sufferings is not about seeking miraculous cures — all cures are anyway miraculous — rather it is about exploring, with the help of visible and tangible reminders, the mystery of suffering. For those who suffer, the wounds of Our Lord's Passion can provide healing for our own invisible wounds — those spiritual traumas inflicted by the sickness itself, as well as the spiritual and emotional damage inflicted by the reactions of others to our situation. When we feel betrayed, Christ's wounds recall to us His constant love; when we suffer loss of identity, they remind us that He chose to suffer for our sakes; when we feel humiliated, we feel the balm of His pity; when we falter under injustice, He gives us the courage to rise and carry on; when we feel tempted to despair, we find consolation in the shadow of the Cross, and hope in the light of the Resurrection.

The Cross reminds us that Jesus was truly man as well as truly God, and felt everything we feel. He founded a Church not solely on speeches and exhortations, with a purely cerebral experience of God, but a Church physical as well as spiritual. He washed the feet of the Disciples and ate and drank with them. He fed the people, healed them, and even raised some from the dead. The Church reflects this emphasis in the genuflection, the sign of the Cross, the anointing, and the laying on of hands; in aural confession and in pilgrimage. As Mother Teresa remarked, 'When you look at the Crucifix, you understand how much Jesus loved you then. When you look at the Sacred Host you understand how much Jesus loves you now'. Christ in the Eucharist—His Body, Blood, Soul and Divinity—under the appearance of food and drink, is the greatest treasure of the Church. Paradoxically, healing for spiritual wounds can be found in all these physical manifestations of spiritual realities.

As the people of the Old Testament offered up their most precious possessions in sacrifice in the quest for spiritual perfection, the Church offers up our sufferings to God, and in the mystery of the Eucharist, offers Christ as the ultimate sacrifice. Jesus offered up His sacred person on the Cross, the culmination of an earthly ministry in which He offered his whole self—Body, Blood, Soul and Divinity—in the service of humanity. Some people wear a bracelet inscribed 'WWJD?'—'What Would Jesus Do?' This helps them follow Jesus in their everyday lives. For Catholics, it should be sufficient to remember Our Lady's words: 'Do whatever he tells you' (Jn 2:5). If we study His words while neglecting His actions we are in danger of neglecting a vital part of His ministry; and in Jesus's healing miracles we discover an exciting and unexpected dimension to His teaching.

Our Lord's healing ministry was often conducted through physical means. For example, when He healed a blind man He made a paste out of spittle and earth and applied it to the man's eyes (Jn 9:1–41). In this age of modern medicine, our first reaction is to recoil from such a 'primitive' act. The earth is something we tend to despise and want to shake off our feet—not so different to the way that the blind man was treated. In making miraculous use of such lowly materials on someone considered by many to be equally lowly, Jesus demonstrated that what is despised by humans is valued by God.

Far from being exotic interludes in His teaching, Our Lord's healing miracles were an intrinsic part of that teaching, illustrating His approach to the sick and the disabled: they mattered. Healing was not just a highly visible aspect of His mission but fundamental to His identity as the Messiah—the Christ. When John the Baptist sent his disciples to enquire whether He was indeed the Messiah, Jesus, quoting from the prophet Isaiah, sent back this message:

> *Go and tell John what you hear and see: the blind receive their sight and the lame walk, lepers are cleansed and the deaf hear, and the dead are raised up, and the poor have good news preached to them. (Mt 11:2–5)*

In studying Christ's healing ministry we see the Kingdom of Heaven fully proclaimed; we see how God the creator responds to the sufferings of His creation, because Jesus was doing His Father's work. (Jn 5:1–18) We also see how our own responses often fall short. *The Five Wounds* explores human suffering in the context of Our Lord's Passion, finding enlightenment and inspiration in both Old and New Testaments. It also points to the practical help found among the treasures of the Church: the sacraments, the teaching and traditions; in popular piety,[56] the visible and tangible reminders of invisible treasures, such as the Rosary, medals and images; the devotion to Our Lady, comfort of the sick and afflicted.[57] The good news is that access to these treasures is not barred to the incapacitated. The Holy Spirit knows no boundaries, and we can join ourselves spiritually to those offering Mass. Prayers and other practical suggestions are given under Resources.

As will be seen in the healing of the woman with the haemorrhage, many people are willing to exploit the sick for their own ends. Others, rather than harmonising their will with God's, as Jesus did when He prayed at Gethsemane, use the plight of the disabled as a showcase for their own healing powers. Under this distorted philosophy the sick and disabled can be made to feel that they somehow lack faith because they have not been cured. This is a gross parody of Our Lord's ministry. Although healing was a fundamental part of it, intrinsic to His salvific mission, He blessed the poor in spirit (Mt 5:3), and when His disciples could not cure a boy suffering from fits, Jesus's impatience was directed not at the afflicted boy, but at those who were unable to help him.[58] Jesus's healing miracles did depend very much on the faith of those asking for help; however, if we took the 'not enough faith' approach to its logical conclusion we would never consult a doctor—an approach that Christians who lecture others on their lack of faith would not themselves take. Most of those whom Jesus cured were too poor to be able to consult a doctor, but doctors cannot always help. Seeking scientific treatments and therapies is not a sign that we lack faith. However, faith can become a problem when it seems there are no cures; then we can become spiritually sick. Jesus healed people spiritually as well as physically.

It can come as a surprise that He asked the sick and disabled what they wanted Him to do for them, but the real surprise is that few people take that trouble. Like the well-meaning Boy Scout they try to help the old lady across the road when she hasn't asked to go. Helping those in need — sensitively, not officiously — is not an 'add on' to Christianity — it is Christianity. We should not expect praise for helping others, or expect thanks for doing our duty (Lk 17: 7–10). St James noted that we tell the needy 'Go in peace, be warmed and filled,' without offering material help; he warned that 'faith by itself, if it has not works, is dead' (Jm 2:14–17). Kind words are better than harsh words, but often they remain just words.

Some politicians claim to support equality for the disabled but also support abortion up to birth for the disabled unborn; some disabled charities dispute about the correct descriptions to apply to disabled people while ignoring the threat to their lives posed by the euthanasia movement; some Christians emphasise the duty to the less able but do not provide disabled access to their churches. In societies where material help is provided by the state, there is sometimes an even greater need for spiritual help. Jesus treated the sick and disabled not just as passive recipients of help but as the possessors of free will — as fully human. The sick also have religious duties: to demonstrate that suffering is not merely negative, to minister to those who minister to us, and to help those who are worse off. In the Jewish faith, even the poor must give alms. Even when we cannot actively help, we can offer up our sufferings for others. This 'apostolate of suffering' was exemplified in the life of Pope John Paul II, who reached out to others despite manifold sufferings; he taught: 'We are not allowed to "pass by on the other side"'.[59]

The Five Wounds, written from the perspective of the sufferer, offers fresh insights into the mystery of suffering. It aims to help those with physical, emotional and mental problems, including 'invisible' sufferings such as depression and phobias, as well as those who help them. The modern approach to sickness too often denies our spiritual dimension, thus ruling out a truly holistic approach—the very approach that Jesus took. In real life, physical suffering is compounded by restricted mobility, difficulties with treatment, or lack of help. Mental and emotional problems often follow physical trauma as the body's store of vital nutrients is depleted. Not all with impairments will be affected all the time, but many will experience episodes of mental, emotional and spiritual difficulties; these include shock, isolation, regret, anger, self-pity, desperation, loss of faith, bitterness, guilt, misery, depression, lethargy, bewilderment, helplessness, resentment, humiliation, and even hatred. Some may even contemplate suicide; a special word is dedicated to them at the conclusion.

When Christ died, He died for all, including those He knew did not believe in Him—even for those who crucified Him; thus *The Five Wounds* is not aimed solely at Christians. However, for sufferers who believe in Him and those who do not, Christ's healing stories make wonderful, joyful sense. He knew, for example, when He forgave the sins of a paralysed man, that he was suffering not just physically but was bearing the whole weight of his history and the spiritual wounds that accompanied it. Jesus saw those invisible wounds. Drawing lessons from His suffering, and with the healing balm of the Church, we can help to heal our own spiritual wounds. This is not escapism: the search for comfort in the wounds of Christ is a flight not from, but to, reality.

Then the eyes of the blind shall be opened, and the ears of the deaf unstopped; then shall the lame man leap like a deer, and the tongue of the mute sing for joy. (Is 35:5–6)

Do not fear, only believe. (Mk 5:36)

Notes

1. In *Salve mundi salutare*, a poem traditionally attributed to St Bernard of Clairvaux (1091–1153) whose stanzas address the various parts of Jesus hanging on the Cross, the final stanza, *Ad faciem*, addresses the face of Jesus; it is known more widely in the English language in Father Ronald Knox's translation as the hymn *O Sacred Head ill-used*, set to the music of J. S. Bach. Ironically, and touchingly, a composition known as the first Lutheran oratorio is *Membra Jesu Nostri* ('The limbs of our Jesus'), by Dieterich Buxtehude in 1680; the aria to the Sacred Head begins 'Hail, bloodied head,/ all crowned with thorns,/ beaten, wounded,/ struck with a cane'. For the Litany of the Sacred Head, see Prayers and Devotions, pp. 102–104 below.
2. E. Duffy, *The Stripping of the Altars: Traditional Religion in England c.1400–c.1580* (Yale University Press: New Haven and London, 1992), pp. 238–248.
3. This was 'said to have been composed by the monks of St Mary's, York' (Letters and Papers of Henry VIII, 1536, no. 787, in D. Mathew, *Catholicism in England 1535–1935: Portrait of a Minority: its Culture and Tradition* (London: The Catholic Book

Club, 1938), pp. 11–13).
4   P. Caraman, *The Western Rising 1549: The Prayer Book Rebellion* (Tiverton, Devon: Westcountry Books, 1999), p. 27.
5   D. Mathew, *Catholicism in England 1535–1935: Portrait of a Minority: its Culture and Tradition* (London: The Catholic Book Club, 1938), pp. 13–14.
6   P. Caraman, *The Western Rising*, p. 60.
7   *Ibid.*, p. 17.
8   *Ibid.*, p. 95.
9   O. Chadwick, *The Reformation* (London: Penguin, 1990), p. 117.
10 Caraman, *The Western Rising*, p. 7.
11 *Ibid.*, p. 129.
12 Quoted in E. P. Thompson, *The Making of the English Working Class* (Harmondsworth, Middlesex: Pelican Books, 1984), p. 408; see also R. A. Knox, *Enthusiasm* (Oxford: OUP, 1950), p. 409. Overlooking Catholic connotations, including echoes of Eucharistic longings, Thompson further quotes: 'We thirst to drink Thy precious blood,/ We languish in Thy wounds to rest,/ And hunger for immortal food,/ And long on all Thy love to feast', commenting: 'This imagery... is subordinated to the overpowering sacrificial imagery of blood, as if the underground traditions of Mithraic blood-sacrifice which troubled the early Christian Church suddenly gushed up in the language of eighteenth-century Methodist hymnody.'
13 R. Taylor, *How to Read a Church* (London: Rider, 2007), p. 94.
14 *Ibid.*, p. 105.
15 *Ibid.*, p. 146.
16 *Ibid.*, p. 112.
17 *Works of Martin Luther* (Philip Melancthon, Wittemburg, 1549). The Reformers excluded any books from their Old Testament that were not included in the Hebrew Bible; this was because they 'were not inclined to accept' those books that suggested it 'was proper to pray for the dead' (A. E. McGrath, *Christian Theology: An Introduction* (Oxford: Blackwell, 1999), pp. 193–194); 'Judaism, according to Luther, was totally preoccupied with the idea of justification by works, believing that it was possible to merit favour in the sight of God by one's achievements. The gospel, in contrast, emphasized that justification was completely gratuitous, resting only on the grace of God'

(p. 197); however, Luther's 'theology of the Cross' emphasised the idea of 'the suffering God' (pp. 250–251).

18 This network also operated abroad: returning to England from the English College in Rome, Father John Gerard's passage through Paris 'was detected and reported to London by one of Walsingham's spies' (P. Caraman, *John Gerard: The Autobiography of an Elizabethan* (London: Longmans, Green and Co., 1951) p. 8 n. 1).

19 Caraman, *The Western Rising*, p. 9.

20 'The first Protestant ruler of England, [the Duke of] Somerset had amassed a huge fortune in monastic lands and on assuming power set about building Somerset House with materials from the old Clerkenwell Priory and the demolished cloister of St Paul's cathedral' (P. Caraman, *The Western Rising* pp. 8–9); Somerset was Lord Protector of England during the reign of Edward VI, until his own downfall in 1549; he was beheaded in 1552.

21 An expression attributed to Irish-American social activist Mary Harris 'Mother' Jones (1837–1930).

22 See: A. G. Dickens, *The Age of Humanism and Reformation* (Milton Keynes, Bucks: Open University Press, 1977).

23 T. R. Malthus, *An Essay on the Principle of Population as It Affects the Future Improvement of Society, with Remarks on the Speculations of Mr Godwin, M. Condorcet, and Other Writers* (London, 1798), available at: http://www.econlib.org/cgi-bin/, at 30 November, 2005. See also G. Talbot Griffiths, *Population Problems of the Age of Malthus* (London: Frank Cass & Co. Ltd., 1926/1967). My father experienced the Workhouse system in the 1920s when he and his brothers were separated from their mother and sisters at the door of the Hackney Workhouse in East London as they awaited admittance.

24 C. Darwin, *On the Origin of Species* (London: Murray, 1859).

25 When Adam and Eve succumbed to the temptation of Satan and disobeyed God's injunction not to eat from the Tree of the knowledge of Good and Evil, 'By refusing God's plan of love, [Man] deceived himself and became a slave to sin. This first alienation engendered a multitude of others. From its outset, human history attests the wretchedness and oppression born of the human heart in consequence of the abuse of freedom' (*Catechism of the Catholic Church*, 1739).

26 C. Darwin, *The Descent of Man* (London: Murray, 1871), quoted in S. Trombley, *The Right to Reproduce: A History of Coercive Sterilization* (London: Weidenfeld & Nicolson, 1988), p. 6.

27 A. McLaren, *Our Own Master Race: Eugenics in Canada 1885–1945* (Toronto: McClelland and Stewart, 1990), p. 17.

28 C. P. Blacker, *Eugenics: Galton and After* (London: Gerald Duckworth, 1952), pp. 65–70.

29 A. Farmer, *By Their Fruits: Eugenics, Population Control, and the Abortion Campaign* (Washington DC: Catholic University of America Press, 2008), pp. 254–270; see also S. Trombley, *The Right to Reproduce: A History of Coercive Sterilization* (London: Weidenfeld & Nicolson, 1988); D. J. Kevles, *In the Name of Eugenics: Genetics and the Uses of Human Heredity* (Cambridge, Mass./London: Harvard University Press, 1995); R. Soloway, *Demography and Degeneration: Eugenics and the Declining Birthrate in Twentieth-Century Britain* (Chapel Hill: University of North Carolina Press, 1995).

30 Among them H. G. Wells (A. Farmer, *By Their Fruits: Eugenics, Population Control, and the Abortion Campaign* (Washington DC: Catholic University of America Press, 2008), pp. 122–127; D. Stone, *Breeding Superman: Nietzsche, Race and Eugenics in Edwardian and Interwar Britain* (Liverpool: Liverpool University Press, 2002).

31 A. Farmer, *By Their Fruits: Eugenics, Population Control, and the Abortion Campaign* (Washington DC: Catholic University of America Press, 2008), pp. 118–122.

32 G. K. Chesterton, 'The Gangster', *G. K.'s Weekly*, August 30, 1934, pp. 408–409.

33 In one of many incidents, in 1939, in the diocese of Münster, Westphalia, a Crucifix was found in pieces on the church floor: 'The figure was missing and was later found hanging by a rope from a tree' (*The Persecution of the Catholic Church in the Third Reich: Facts and Documents* (London: Burns Oates, 1940), pp. 544–549).

34 *The Persecution of the Catholic Church in the Third Reich: Facts and Documents* (London: Burns Oates, 1940), pp. 121–127; 247–248.

35 'The huge volume of "No Popery" literature in the nineteenth century indicated clearly—as Newman pointed out —that

Catholicism was "the victim of a prejudice which perpetuates itself and gives birth to what it feeds upon"' (J. H. Newman, *Lectures on the Present Position of Catholics in England* (1851/1892), in E. R. Norman, *Anti-Catholicism in Victorian England* (London: George Allen and Unwin Ltd., 1968), pp. 13–14).

36 G. K. Chesterton, *The Catholic Church and Conversion* (San Francisco: Ignatius Press, 1926/2006), pp. 21–25. 'The world still pays us this wild and imaginative compliment of imagining that we are much less ordinary than we really are. ... ...Roman Catholics do not generally shout to each other the arrangements of a St Bartholomew Massacre across the public streets; and the only deduction any reasonable man can draw is that they do it behind closed doors' (G. K. Chesterton, *The Thing* (London: Sheed & Ward, 1929), p. 140).

37 The Voluntary Euthanasia Society was launched in 1936; Dame Cicely Saunders (1918–2005) established the purpose-built St Christopher's Hospice in South London, in 1967.

38 For example, in *Macbeth*, Lady Macbeth complains that her husband, though ambitious, is 'too full o' th' milk of human kindness to catch the greatest way' (W. Shakespeare, *Macbeth*, Act I, Scene V, *William Shakespeare: the Complete Works* (London: Collins, 1970), p. 1003); Shakespeare introduced the idea of Purgatory in his use of ghostly characters, as when the ghost of Banquo enters the feast and sits in the place of Macbeth, who ordered his murder (W. Shakespeare, *Macbeth*, Act III, Scene IV, *William Shakespeare: the Complete Works* (London: Collins, 1970), p. 1013); however, the play, written in the same year as the Gunpowder Plot, also contained a warning to Catholics goaded to extreme action by persecution (C. Asquith, *Shadowplay: the Hidden Beliefs and Coded Politics of William Shakespeare* (New York: Public Affairs, 2005), pp. 212–222).

39 *Little Dorrit* (1855–57) features Maggy, a mentally disabled young woman; *Our Mutual Friend* (1864–65) features tiny Jenny Wren, a heroic dolls' dressmaker, and Sloppy, the loyal and enthusiastic mangling assistant; the tragic Smike is a major character in *Nicolas Nickleby* (1838–39); *Dombey and Son* (1846–48) describes the life and death of the sickly little Paul Dombey; in *A Christmas Carol* (1843) Tiny Tim, the little disabled son of Bob Cratchit, is eventually cured through

Scrooge's change of heart; even the villainous dwarf Quilp in *The Old Curiosity Shop* (1841) is more human than Mrs Quilp's mother, who 'sold' her daughter in marriage to Quilp, and more honest than her friends, who accept the Quilps' hospitality but criticise Quilp behind his back.

40   '"Bah!' said Scrooge. 'Humbug!"' (C. Dickens, *A Christmas Carol* (1843) *Best Ghost Stories* (Ware, Herts: Wordsworth Classics, 1997), p. 60); G. K. Chesterton, 'Dickens and Christmas', *Charles Dickens* (London: Methuen & Co. Ltd., 1906/1913), pp. 118–135.

41   C. Dickens, *A Christmas Carol* (1843) *Best Ghost Stories* (Ware, Herts: Wordsworth Classics, 1997), p. 63.

42   'The air was filled with phantoms, wandering hither and thither in restless haste, and moaning as they went. Every one of them wore chains like Marley's Ghost; some few (they might be guilty governments) were linked together; none were free. Many had been personally known to Scrooge in their lives. He had been quite familiar with one old ghost in a white waistcoat, with a monstrous iron safe attached to its ankle, who cried piteously at being unable to assist a wretched woman with an infant, whom it saw below upon a doorstep. The misery with them all was clearly that they sought to interfere, for good, in human matters, and had lost the power for ever' (C. Dickens, *A Christmas Carol* (1843) *Best Ghost Stories* (Ware, Herts: Wordsworth Classics, 1997), p. 72).

43   See J. Uglow, *William Hogarth: A Life and a World* (London: Faber & Faber, 2002).

44   Written as a preface to *Milton, a Poem, Jerusalem* was set to music by Sir Hubert Parry in 1916 and is a favourite at the BBC's *Last Night of the Proms* broadcast each year in September: 'I will not cease from Mental Fight,/ Nor shall my Sword sleep in my hand:/ Till we have built Jerusalem,/ In England's green & pleasant Land'.

45   G. K. Chesterton, *A Short History of England* (London: Chatto & Windus, 1917), p. 149.

46   W. Cobbett, *A History of the Protestant Reformation in England and Ireland* (London: Catholic Publishing & Bookselling Company, Limited, n.d.), p. 3.

47   The 'medieval' idea influenced the Gothic revival architecture of A. W. N. Pugin, and the art and politics of William Morris

and John Ruskin, as well as Edwardian anti-capitalists including G. K. Chesterton and Hilaire Belloc; the idea also influenced historical interpretation: the Christian Socialist historian R. H. Tawney's *Religion and the Rise of Capitalism* (1926) agreed with Weber's theory of the Protestant work ethic; it was followed by Herbert Butterfield's influential *The Whig Interpretation of History* (1931); see: G. K. Chesterton, 'William Morris and his School', *Twelve Types* (Norfolk, VA: IHS Press, 1902/2003), pp. 16–21; J. P. McCarthy, *Hilaire Belloc: Edwardian Radical* (Indianapolis: Liberty Press, 1978); M. Alexander, *Medievalism: the Middle Ages in modern England* (London/New Haven, CO: Yale University Press, 2007).

48 A nurse with almost 30 years' service, Shirley Chaplin, was threatened with disciplinary action after refusing to remove a necklace bearing a Cross as a symbol of her deeply held religious beliefs, after National Health Service managers insisted that the Cross must be removed from sight, as part of their uniform policy, and as a health risk to her and to patients. Another Christian nurse was suspended from work for offering to pray for an elderly patient, and faced dismissal for breaching their code of conduct on equality and diversity (*Christian Concern* website, 21 September 2009, available at: www.christianconcern.com on 5 October 2011).

49 Doctors were forced to prescribe drinking water for elderly NHS hospital patients to stop them dying of thirst, in order to remind nurses 'of the most basic necessity'; investigations showed that 'staff routinely ignored patients' calls for help and forgot to check that they had had enough to eat and drink'; the deaths of more than 800 hospital patients every year are associated with dehydration; a further 300 die malnourished; a report by the official inspectors, the Care Quality Commission, found that a quarter of the NHS hospital trusts they had visited in the previous three months 'were failing to meet the most basic standards required by law'; some wards could face closure for 'neglecting the elderly on such a fundamental level' (*Daily Mail*, 27 May 2011, available at: http://www.dailymail.co.uk, on 6 October 2011).

50 The National Institute for Health and Clinical Excellence (NICE) decides which drugs can be used on NHS patients, based on cost and the value to patients, for example cancer drugs that extend the lives of terminally ill patients; at the

same time, drugs bills, footed by the taxpayer, have rocketed ('"NHS doesn't care about cost of medicine": Drugs firms accused of profiteering by raising prices by one thousand per cent', *Daily Mail*, 18 July, 2010, available at Mail Online, at: http://www.dailymail.co.uk, on 5 October 2011). See Chapter Four note 1.

51 Penicillin was discovered by Alexander Fleming in 1928; as well as the over-prescribing of antibiotics, poor hygiene in hospitals has been blamed for the spread of antibiotic resistant strains of bacteria, prompting a campaign to promote handwashing in hospitals; there is now a 'Global Handwashing Day' (October 15).

52 Under the European Directive on Traditional Herbal Medicinal Products (THMPD) all herbal medicinal products are required to obtain an authorisation in order to be sold within the European Union; after a transitional period, all such products, some of them in use for hundreds or even thousands of years, must be licensed by the EU to ensure their safety, a costly process that will drive up the cost of more popular products, while lesser-used products may become unavailable (Adam Smith, 'Doing the avoidance waltz with the European Commission', Alliance for Natural Health, available at: http://www.anh-europe.org, at 5 October, 2011).

53 Screened in November 1966, *Cathy Come Home* was watched by 12 million viewers, prompting a surge in support for the newly formed homelessness charity Shelter, founded by the Rev. Bruce Kenrick ('Shelter: Our History', available at: http://www.england.shelter.org.uk, on 7 October 2011).

54 Live Aid was founded by singer Bob Geldof after watching the BBC reporter Michael Buerk reporting from Ethiopia ('BBC Home: On This Day', available at: http://www.bbc.news.co.uk, on 7 October 2011).

55 'Secret Court of Protection can order abortions and sterilisations of mentally ill patients', Daily Telegraph, 28 May 2010.

56 *Catechism of the Catholic Church*, 1674–1676.

57 See Prayers and Devotions, pp. 95 ff. below.

58 The boy is described as being possessed by a spirit that threw him into convulsions, making him foam at the mouth. Belief in evil spirits sometimes overlapped with physical disease. Jesus upheld such ideas, but also addressed the physical

problem; in this case, He 'rebuked the unclean spirit and cured the boy' (Lk 9:37–43).

59   Pope John Paul II, Apostolic letter *Salvifici Doloris* (On the Christian Meaning of Human Suffering), 1984.

Chapter One

Betrayed

All who hate me whisper together about me ...
Even my bosom friend in whom I trusted, who
ate of my bread, has lifted his heel against me.
(Ps 41)

If there is anything worse than betrayal by one's enemies, it is betrayal by one's friends. Many fears and phobias are caused by the breaking of trust, starting when a baby is surrendered by its parents to the nurse who administers a painful injection. When we need help most, we feel abandoned as old friends lose touch, and opportunities to make new friendships are restricted. As our physical and mental abilities desert us, we can even feel betrayed by our own bodies.

In the Bible, Job, a righteous man, is afflicted with many dreadful physical complaints. His friends, rather than sympathising, suggest that his problems are caused by sin. In the secular world, we seem beset by 'Job's comforters' suggesting that our lifestyles and mental attitudes are at fault, and that all we need to overcome our problems is a positive attitude; as Mrs Chick advises her dying sister-in-law in Dickens's *Dombey and Son*, all we require is a little more effort. [1] Some Christians will suggest that we haven't enough faith. Perhaps the truth is that we are testing their faith by not getting better; but with such doubts sown in our minds, we may begin to doubt our own judgement; we may find our self-trust deserting us just when we need it most.

A common response to emotional and spiritual trauma is to guard ourselves against further 'betrayals'. We avoid people that have hurt us; we avoid placing ourselves in someone else's power. However, when we need to rely on someone for treatment or care, panic sets in as we realise that our life is not in our own hands. The instinct of self-preservation can overwhelm even our trust in God.

> *And as they were eating he said, 'Truly, I say to you, one of you will betray me.' (Mt 26:21–22)*

Jesus was betrayed not only by His enemies, but also — though they repented — by His friends. Despite their commitment to Him, and despite Our Lord's commitment to their welfare, 'they all deserted him and fled' (Mk 14:50).

Our Lord's response to betrayal by His enemies was to surrender Himself to God's will, in the shape of the Roman soldiers. When they asked for 'Jesus the Nazarene', He replied, 'I told you that I am he; so, if you seek me, let these men go' (Jn 18:8). In doing His Father's will Jesus spared the friends He knew would desert Him.

A Healing Ministry

Martha and Mary sent a message to Jesus, who was staying some distance away, to say that their brother Lazarus was ill; however, Jesus, despite His close friendship with the little family, remained where He was for two more days, telling His disciples, 'Lazarus is dead...' He then set out on to perform the ultimate healing miracle—to restore Lazarus to life (Jn 11:1–44).

Look at the birds of the air: they neither sow nor reap nor gather into barns, and yet your heavenly Father feeds them. Are you not of more value than they? (Mt 6:25–34)

Jesus did not go straightaway to heal Lazarus, despite their friendship; it must have seemed almost like a betrayal to Martha and Mary. When at last He arrived, Mary said, 'Lord, if you had been here, my brother would not have died'. But Jesus told His Disciples, 'for your sake I am glad that I was not there, so that you may believe'; He told Martha, 'Did I not tell you that if you would believe you would see the glory of God?' (Jn 11:1–44). However, on encountering Mary's distress and the grief of those who came to comfort her, He was profoundly affected; He wept. As man, Jesus truly shared His friends' sufferings and their bereavement, even though, as God, He could see the joyful outcome.

The resurrection of Lazarus was accomplished so the Disciples would believe in Jesus, not to indicate that they would be invincible. Jesus prepared them for their coming trials, especially Peter, warning him, 'When you are old, you will stretch out your hands, and another will fasten your belt for you and carry you where you do not wish to go'. Still He added, 'Follow me' (Jn 21:15–19). The Disciples would not be invincible, but they would not be alone. They would be following even more closely in the Master's footsteps, for Jesus also warned them of His coming passion, death and resurrection (Mt 16:21–23). Yet he told them, 'Do not fear those who kill the body but cannot kill the soul; rather fear him who can destroy both soul and body in hell.' Such solemn warnings came with an assurance—they could trust in God.

Even the hairs of your head are all numbered.
(Mt 10:28–31)

Like the Disciples we fear an unknown future, based on past 'betrayals'. Jesus trusted in His Father; He told Pilate, 'You would have no power over me unless it had been given you from above…' (Jn 19:11). We need to know that when we put ourselves in the hands of others, we are really placing ourselves in the hands of God.

Healing Balm from the Church

Judas betrayed God but he perished because he could not trust in God's forgiveness (Mt 27:3–5); God betrays no one. No one who has said in desperation, 'God, if you're there, help me…' has slipped from His hands. We may have failed to trust Him; we may even, by implication, blame Him for our plight. We may have stayed away from the Sacrament of Reconciliation because, like Shakespeare's King Lear, we feel 'more sinned against than sinning'. Fewer people avail themselves of this Sacrament nowadays; but rather than a sign that we are becoming perfect, it may be that we do not recognise our own need for it.

> *Forgive us our trespasses, as we forgive those who trespass against us... (Mt 6:12)*

In instituting the Eucharist, Jesus made His eternal commitment to us in the most physical of ways, by giving us His body and blood. He strengthens our commitment to Him physically as well as spiritually by becoming part of us, renewing us day by day, as long as our lives remain open to Him. He will never desert us, even to death.

> *Thanks be to God for trusting us when we lose trust in Him.*

Pray for friends, especially those who have lost touch. Do they need our help? Ask Our Lady, who never deserted her Son, even unto death (Jn 19:25–27), to help us remain true to Him. Watch and pray before the Blessed Sacrament, as Jesus asked His Disciples to do on the night He was betrayed, that we may regain our trust in our one true friend, and never again desert Him.

> *God of constant love, I praise you.*

Our Lord trusted Peter, even when Peter could not trust Our Lord. Ask St Peter—who unlike Judas, repented and followed Jesus to become the first pope, even to martyrdom—for the courage to commit our lives to Jesus. In an age when everyone is looking for commitment, but few are willing to commit, pray that we may truly commit to those whose trust has been betrayed.

> *The Lord is a stronghold for the oppressed, a stronghold in times of trouble. And those who*

know your name put their trust in you, for you, O Lord, have not forsaken those who seek you. (Ps 9)

And behold, I am with you always, to the close of the age. (Jn 14:1)

Notes

1 '[Y]ou may rest assured that there is nothing wanting but an effort on Fanny's part. And that effort,' she continued, taking off her bonnet, and adjusting her cap and gloves, in a businesslike manner, 'she must be encouraged, and really, if necessary, urged to make' (C. Dickens, *Dombey and Son* (Ware, Herts: Wordsworth Classics, 1995), p. 12.

Chapter Two

Who am I?

But I am a worm, and no man; scorned by men, and despised by the people. (Ps 22)

Sickness, disability and depression can be accompanied by loss of identity as we feel we can no longer trust in our selves; unable to do the things we want, or even need to do, feelings of self-worth can be dented, leading to severe loss of confidence. At the very time when we most need help, we find it difficult to summon up the spiritual strength to explain our needs. The fear of being, or of becoming, a burden to others—exacerbated by calls for euthanasia—is very real.

Struggling with physical or mental impairment is a daily challenge under which we can feel like a cork tossed about in a rough sea, sometimes without enough energy to ride the next wave. Relationships, even with God, can come under strain. We feel exhausted and afraid, only too willing to clutch at offers of help, even if it means surrendering what we feel to be our true identity; by becoming what others see us to be. In a world that defines us by what we do rather than who we are, we become a patient, a client, a case to be dealt with; a number on a list. Or we can simply become invisible.

Pilate said to him, 'So you are a king?' (Jn 18:37)

Pilate, governor of Judaea, was keenly interested in the political implications of a Jewish king, and the threat to his ability to control this turbulent yet strategic corner of the Roman Empire. Jesus knew that He was the Son of God, the promised Messiah, but His revelation of this status was related to the ability of His hearers to absorb its cataclysmic import. Jesus had asked the Disciples, 'Who do men say that the Son of man is?' (Mt 16:13). When at Capernaum 'an unclean spirit' afflicting a man shouted 'I know who you are: the Holy One of God', Jesus rebuked it (Mk 1:21–28). Jesus was not unsure of His own identity; He wanted to be recognised—but not as a result of malicious and premature revelation. Moreover, He invited people to recognise Him, rather than forcing them to acknowledge His reign, as human rulers did. When Jesus had miraculously fed five thousand people, and they were 'about to come and take him by force to make him king', He 'withdrew again to the hills by himself' (Jn 6:14–15). Under Pilate's interrogation, He did not at once reveal His identity or try to sway the cynical Roman governor by clever argument; instead Jesus gave Pilate the opportunity to recognise the spiritual nature of His realm: 'My kingship is not of this world...' (Jn 18:36). He allowed even Pilate the chance to be saved. In proclaiming His status as Son of God, Jesus demonstrated care for fragile human faith, and respect for the free will with which He endowed all human beings.

Jesus did not use miracles to force people to believe. Although, as with Lazarus, He performed miracles to strengthen the faith of His followers, and sometimes emphasised this point when healing the sick, mostly He healed people simply because they asked Him. When a leper said to Jesus, 'Lord, if you will, you can make me clean', Jesus replied, 'I will; be clean' (Mt 8:1–4). Jesus was only too ready to heal people, but He would not heal people against their will; there had to be a degree of faith. Some people were positively hostile: the people from His neighbourhood were sceptical of Jesus, and became so angry that they tried to throw Him over a cliff (Lk 4:28–30). He did not use supernatural means to force them to acknowledge Him; He 'did not do many mighty works there, because of their unbelief' (Mt 13:58). Jesus did not insist on a firm belief in Him before He would perform miracles, but there had to be an openness to belief; people had to be ready to 'take a chance' on Him, even if their faith was born of desperation. When a boy suffering from fits and thought to be possessed by a spirit was brought to Jesus by his father, Jesus told him: 'All things are possible to him who believes'. The father, clearly at the end of his tether because his son had often fallen into the fire and into water, burst out: 'I believe; help my unbelief!' (Mk 9:14–29).

A Healing Ministry

Our Lord's version of kingliness—humble service, rather than arrogant force—was reflected in His approach to the sick and disabled. It can be seen most clearly in His response to a woman with an embarrassing, debilitating and socially isolating complaint (Mk 5:21–34; Lk 8:43–48). She had suffered from a haemorrhage for twelve years, and came to Jesus through the crowd; without speaking, she 'touched his garment'. Her humiliation was compounded by the fact that she had 'suffered much under many physicians, and had spent all that she had, and was no better but rather grew worse'. Her desperation produced a miracle unique among those described in the Gospels. Jesus knew that 'power had gone forth from him', and 'immediately' the woman was cured. He had healed someone without being asked—in words, at least. This is itself remarkable; what is just as remarkable is that Jesus demanded to know who had touched Him. His bewildered Disciples pointed out that the crowd was pressing around Him, but Jesus persisted. The woman came forward 'in fear and trembling'; her complaint had caused her to be ritually unclean, thus she must have experienced acute social isolation for many years. Now, she anticipated a rebuke for transgressing religious laws that required her to keep herself apart from society (Lv 15:25–27).

Behold, I have graven you on the palms of my hands… (Is 49:16)

No such rebuke came. Jesus had been on His way to heal the daughter of Jairus, the president of the local synagogue, but in His humility he stopped to help the woman who humbly touched His garment; He already knew her story, but singled her out so that the world could hear it: 'Daughter, your faith has made you well; go in peace and be healed of your disease'. Society had relegated the woman to a lowly position because of her illness, shattering her feelings of self-worth; Jesus elevated her to the highest position because of her faith, reaffirming her identity as a child of God.

Healing Balm from the Church

A humble God refuses to force Himself on mankind, but offers Himself freely, taking a chance on our rejection. Like the Nazarenes, it is possible to be so familiar with Jesus that we fail to recognise Him as Christ the King. In the Sacrament of Reconciliation, we can once again acknowledge His reign in our lives; in the face of His humility, we confess our own shortcomings.

> *Forgive us our trespasses, as we forgive those who trespass against us... (Mt 6:12)*

Jesus put His body at the disposal of the needy, and allowed His healing powers to go out to the sick. In the Eucharist, in the midst of a crowd, we can experience healing from His body, blood, soul and divinity, for our body and blood; for our heart, mind and spirit.

> *Thanks be to God for seeing me worthy of redemption; thanks be to Jesus for choosing to suffer for me.*

Pray that we may confidently claim our true identity as children of God. Pray for the confidence to proclaim our selves followers of Jesus, to wear a blessed crucifix or Miraculous Medal[1] as a sign of that discipleship—something we can touch whenever confidence is needed.

> *God of humility, I praise you.*

When experiencing loss of identity, ask St Martha, who unhesitatingly affirmed her belief in the identity of

Jesus as the Christ, to help us make the same affirmation. (Jn 11:25–27) Ask St Mary, who listened at the feet of Christ (Lk 10:38–42) to help us listen patiently and sensitively to the needs of others, as God listens to us. Ask Our Lady, who was alert to the needs of others, as at the Wedding Feast at Cana, (Jn 2: 1–3) not to be so absorbed in our own troubles that we forget the needs of the needy.

For you formed my inward parts, you knitted me together in my mother's womb. (Ps 139)

Are not five sparrows sold for two pennies? And not one of them is forgotten before God. Fear not; you are of more value than many sparrows. (Lk 12:6–7)

Notes

[1] Our Lady described the design of the Miraculous Medal when she appeared to St Catherine Labouré, a French nun, in Paris in 1830; it was to bear her image and the inscription 'O Mary, conceived without sin, pray for us who have recourse to thee'; this referred to the belief in the Immaculate Conception, proclaimed as dogma by Pope Pius IX in 1854; see *Catechism of the Catholic Church*, 490–494.

Chapter Three

Why Me?

I am poured out like water, and all my bones are out of joint; my heart is like wax, it is melted within my breast; my strength is dried up like a potsherd, and my tongue cleaves to my jaws; you lay me in the dust of death. (Ps 22)

Strangely enough, the experience of incapacity can make us feel unjustly treated. Although we can rationalise other people's misfortunes, somehow we see an ethical dimension to our own; they seem not just unfortunate but 'wrong'.

Without realising it, by dwelling on what has happened to us, we can build our own memorial to this perceived injustice. We can build on it by perceiving injustice in other people's reactions to our plight, and pile it even higher with our resentment against them. By spending the 'now' in memorialising the injustices of the past, we starve the spirit, walling it up in a sepulchre built with our own hands. We may say that we can forgive but not forget—but is this forgiveness authentic? At the Devil's prompting it is easy to join the 'victim culture' that sees everyone else as oppressors. We may not recognise what we are doing because rather than 'taking it to the Lord in prayer' we may hide such resentments from Him, failing to mention the biggest thing on our minds. Thus we end up feeling angry and resentful towards God who is the author of all things.

> *They led him out to crucify him. And they compelled a passer-by, Simon of Cyrene, who was coming in from the country, the father of Alexander and Rufus, to carry his cross. (Mk 15:20–21)*

Tradition tells us Jesus fell three times on the way to His crucifixion and this is represented in the Stations of the Cross. The Roman soldiers ordered Simon of Cyrene, possibly visiting Jerusalem for the Passover, to help Jesus (Mk 15:21–22). This was not done out of compassion. These most efficient and cruel of executioners wanted to ensure that their victims did not die before they could kill them. Outside Jerusalem, on a hill specially selected as a warning, the occupied Jewish people would have to pass the ghastly sight of crucified men on their way in and out of the city, each one with a notice of their crimes pinned above them. Crucifixion was designed to maximise the suffering of the victim, and a fall on the way provided the soldiers with the opportunity to inflict further cruelty. They forced Jesus to get up and carry on, although eventually His poor physical state prompted their conscription of Simon. Jesus had been without sleep for over twenty-four hours; in the garden of Gethsemane He spent time in fervent prayer while His Disciples slept.

He had been dragged from Pilate to Herod and back again. He had been scourged and beaten, with much loss of blood. But even before this, His public ministry had been met by unjust treatment: so great were the demands on Him for teaching and healing that He often sought time alone to pray (Mt 14:23; Mk 1:35; Lk 5:16). Even Our Lord's healing miracles had not always been received with thanks, most famously when He healed a group of ten lepers, of whom only one returned to thank Him (Lk 17:11–19). In His hour of need His friends deserted Him.

When the Roman soldiers and Temple guards, led by Judas, arrived to arrest Jesus, Simon Peter drew his sword and cut off the ear of Malchus, the High Priest's servant. Jesus told Peter to put his sword away, and at once healed the man (Jn 18:1–11). When He fell on the way to execution Jesus got up again to continue His journey to Calvary. On the Cross, rather than protesting at the injustice done to Him—which even one of the crucified thieves acknowledged—Jesus said, 'Father, forgive them; for they know not what they do' (Lk 23:35–43).

A Healing Ministry

Our Lord's justice was quite different to human justice. When, at the Temple, the Disciples saw the man who had been born blind they asked, 'Rabbi, who sinned, this man or his parents, that he was born blind?' Jesus said: 'It was not that this man sinned, or his parents, but that the works of God might be made manifest in him'. Jesus healed the man and later sought him out after he had been ejected from the Temple for robustly defending the act of healing from the criticism of the Temple authorities. In this instance Jesus sought evidence of faith after a healing, asking him: 'Do you believe in the Son of man?' Moreover, in a scathing commentary on human views of disability, He told those who criticised Him for working on the Sabbath: 'If you were blind, you would have no guilt; but now that you say, "We see," your guilt remains' (Jn 9:1–41).

Nonetheless, Jesus appeared to display unjust attitudes in the case of the Syro-Phoenician woman; she begged Him to help her daughter, 'possessed by an unclean spirit'. Clearly embarrassed by the woman's noisy entreaties, the Disciples urged Jesus to grant her request—her shouts were drawing attention to His presence in the region of Tyre, where He was attempting to stay quietly. Unusually, Jesus ignored the woman's pleading, eventually telling her: 'I was sent only to the lost sheep of the house of Israel'. Bowing low, she reiterated her request but He responded: 'It is not fair to take the children's bread and throw it to the dogs'. Undeterred, the woman swiftly turned the tables on Jesus: 'Yes, Lord; yet even the dogs under the table eat the children's crumbs'. Just as swiftly Jesus praised her: 'O woman, great is your faith! Let it be done for you as you desire'; her daughter was 'healed instantly' (Mt 15:21–28; Mk 7:24–30). He appeared to enjoy this kind of banter, even with women.[1] Seemingly able to read people's minds, He knew she was a woman of faith, and not shy of speaking out. He also knew when people were being insincere, and His response was to tease out the truth. He took this approach to the feisty Syro-Phoenician woman—but His apparent injustice to her was designed to tease out the truth from the Disciples, who had only wanted Him to help the woman to stop her from disturbing their peace. In appearing to ignore her, Jesus provoked her into making a public profession of faith, and it was her faith that impressed Him. Moreover, as well as praising her faith, in His ultimate response to the woman He was able to teach that gentiles were not outside the scheme of God's salvation. Some gentiles were referred to as 'dogs', and Jews generally took care not to venture into Samaritan territory (Jn 4:9), but Jesus's use of the term 'little dogs', the woman's ready reply—she was clearly emboldened rather than crushed by His attitude—and His delight in her response, suggest that He used the encounter to criticise injustice, not to commit injustice. On another occasion, He sought an encounter with a Samaritan woman specifically to encourage her faith, and that of her community (Jn 4:1–42). He also told the parable of the Good Samaritan to challenge people's prejudices about others (Lk 10:25–37). By openly voicing such hidden prejudices He was teaching the Disciples—and us—a lesson in justice.

> *For you have maintained my just cause; you have sat on the throne giving righteous judgement. (Ps 9)*

Nonetheless, Our Lord's teaching on justice can appear confusing. He said, 'Love your enemies and pray for those who persecute you' (Mt 5:44); He called 'those who hunger and thirst for righteousness' blessed, along with 'the peacemakers' (Mt 5:1–10). Despite this He said: 'I have not come to bring peace, but a sword'; (Mt 10:34–35) at the Last Supper He asked the Disciples if they had any swords (Lk 22:35–38); but when the soldiers came to arrest Him He told Peter to put away his sword and healed the high priest's servant. Jesus taught: 'To him who strikes you on the cheek, offer the other also' (Lk 6:27–35), but when slapped by an officer of the High Priest for speaking up He answered: 'If I have spoken wrongly, bear witness to the wrong; but if I have spoken rightly, why do you strike me?' (Jn 18:12–24) Although Jesus does not retaliate against the unjust action of the guard, neither does He accept the injustice. Pointing out the guard's sin was an act of love, since his immortal soul was in danger. Nonetheless the innocent Jesus endured the injustice, and in so doing saved the world.[2] In enduring injustice for the sake of doing God's will, the innocent sufferer of sickness or disability is not concurring in the unjust verdict, delivered by some, that he or she is worthless or burdensome; to do so would lead to depression and low self-esteem, increasing the temptation to suicide. Rather, it is saying: 'You are wrong—I am not worthless—but neither are you; we both need to be saved'. Our Lord addressed issues of justice in His healing ministry, making clear that although deliberately inflicted suffering is sinful, sickness is not a punishment from God. Sickness is not a moral failing, but it does have a 'meaning', and we continue to search for that meaning. Our search inevitably leads back to God, the author of all things. Even if He does not will our suffering, we believe He could remove it if He wanted to, thus—since God is just—sickness still feels like a punishment.

> *He was oppressed, and he was afflicted, yet he opened not his mouth... (Is 53:7)*

The problem and mystery of the innocent man who suffers is explored in the Bible, which describes how Job, a righteous man, was afflicted with much physical suffering. Certain of his innocence, he refused to confess his sins, showing his resentment against God. Seen in a purely negative light, suffering can provoke resentment, but embraced as a vocation it can be transformed into something positive, as John Paul II demonstrated in his pontificate. Indeed, the adversity he suffered in his life shaped the man he was—the right man at the right time to do the job God wanted to be done. The last link in the chain was supplied by John Paul himself—his permission. Like all living things in the material world, no human growth can occur without change; indeed, Jesus, 'the Vine', described His Father as 'the vinedresser. Every branch of mine that bears no fruit, he takes away, and every branch that does bear fruit he prunes, that it may bear more fruit' (Jn 15: 1–2). To take a modern analogy, God is like an employer with several urgent jobs awaiting attention; but He never forces anyone to take on a job. In sickness and disability we come into contact with people we would probably never have met had we chosen our own route in life rather than finding ourselves on the rocky road of suffering. Far from punishing us, God is entrusting us with a very precious responsibility, the opportunity to help others. It is a vocation—should we choose to accept it. In the end Job bowed to God's will in enduring the suffering he could not understand; but the true exemplar of the righteous man is Jesus, the Suffering Servant (Is 53), who in his response to injustice goes to the heart of the mystery of human suffering. He suffered evil without complaint, because His suffering was an intrinsic part of His Father's plan for mankind's salvation. Our Lord's warning that violence would result from the Prince of Peace's intervention in human affairs was a paradox illustrated by His own treatment: the man who offered no resistance to injustice, the innocent man, was crucified, while the guilty Barabbas readily accepted his freedom.

The feeling that things are 'wrong'—from individual illness to natural disasters—and our yearning for them to be 'put right', are signs of our spiritual heritage—our yearning for the Garden of Eden. This feeling is confirmed in Our Lord's healing ministry. Without blaming people for sickness or disability—or excusing them from responsibility for their attitudes to their situations either—he restored them to their natural state, health.

Healing Balm from the Church

Often we say prayers for specific intentions, and that is good. But when we are suffering, we can offer up the suffering as a prayer. Moreover, it is unfettered prayer, like making a donation to a charity and allowing it to be used wherever it is most needed. Unfettered by our specific request, our suffering can give God 'permission' to intervene in people's lives even when no petition has been received by Him; for example, from individuals in great need—perhaps babies or little children; those who do not know God, or may have been turned against Him by the poor example of others—all those on whose behalf no one has asked for Divine help. Unfettered prayer is a prayer for God's intentions. Once, when due to have a gastric exploration in hospital, I was very anxious, and offered up the anxiety for someone due to undergo an abortion. When I woke up I found they had been unable to do the exploration because I kept pulling out the gastric tube. At first I was disappointed, but was consoled by the thought that perhaps someone, somewhere, had changed her mind about having an abortion. God is Love, and love is self-giving. This is the mystery of suffering, because although weakness is despised by the powerful, love, not power, is the currency of the Universe: God can bring good out of evil, therefore suffering is not worthless but valuable, because unlike the currencies of the world we can exchange something bad for something good. In some cases it can be a fantastically good exchange rate: my small pain in exchange for sparing a helpless person from some dreadful evil; for allowing a human being to be born. It can even relieve our suffering to offer it up, but when things are really bad, and we cannot think of any other prayer to pray, we can say, 'Father, bring good out of this evil'. The God who brought life out of death is the only one who can do this, although we may never see the results in this life. Jesus told His followers that when they were fasting they should not walk around with long faces (Mt 6:16) and when we offer up sufferings we must do it cheerfully because we are doing it for God; a grudging helper has already taken back what he or she offered up to Him.

Indeed, we can't be true followers of Jesus, the 'Way', if we don't follow His way—the narrow way of suffering. The Disciples learnt this only too well, and St. Paul speaks in detail of his own sufferings in spreading the Gospel; however, 'as we share abundantly in Christ's sufferings, so through Christ we shared abundantly in comfort too' (2 Co 1:5). When we suffer injustice, we often try to find the broad short-cut to happiness, but that way 'leads to destruction'; in contrast, the way to life 'is narrow and the way is hard... and those who find it are few' (Mt 7:13–14). It can be painful to have to give way to others, and when we are thrust aside we can waste time and energy in bitterness and anger; in nursing grudges; in minimising other people's claims to justice. Instead of seeing our faith in God as a preparation for adversity, we see the adversity as a betrayal of our faith in God. Like the nine lepers who forgot to say thank you to Jesus we forget the good things and cling on to the bad. Before long such feelings form an obstacle between us and our Father in Heaven. We are faced with a choice: to remove the obstacle and be reunited with God in the Sacrament of Reconciliation, thus handing over our cause to the only truly just judge; or we can cling on to the sins and take them with us into eternity (Mt 5:29–30; Mk 9:43–48).

> *Forgive us our trespasses, as we forgive those who trespass against us... (Mt 6:12)*

Only when truly reconciled with God can we truly receive the body and blood of His Son in the Eucharist. His crucified body can strengthen us to accept the spiritual wounds, as He accepted the nails that were hammered into his flesh; we can bathe our wounds in the mercy flowing from His unjustly inflicted wounds.

> *Thanks be to God for tempering justice with mercy.*

Pray for all those we meet along the rocky road — especially those who elbow us out of the way. Pray that rather than feeling anger or shame, we can see our suffering as part of God's plan of salvation. Pray for the courage to forgive injustice done to us, and to refrain from inflicting it; pray that we will share the burdens of those who are denied justice, especially those who cannot defend themselves; pray for the courage to rise, pick up the cross and carry on when we fall. When we are unfairly treated, or tormented by memories of unjust treatment, the Stations of the Cross show us how Christ the perfect victim gave Himself to be victimised for the sake of all victims, and all victimisers; how He fell again and again, but got up to complete the journey for our sakes.

God of true justice, I praise you.

Ask Simon of Cyrene for help when it is most needed: for the next step of the journey. When falsely accused or unfairly treated, ask the Holy Spirit to be our advocate. (Jn 14:16) Ask Our Lady, who in the Stations of the Cross meets her Son on His way to execution—who witnessed His unjust treatment—to help us feel sorrow for all victims and all victimisers, and to pray for them.

Vindicate me, O Lord, for I have walked in my integrity, and I have trusted in the Lord without wavering. (Ps 26)

In the world you have tribulation; but be of good cheer, I have overcome the world. (Jn 16:33)

Notes

[1] For example, his exchange with a woman in the crowd (Lk 11:27–28), his unembarrassed response to the woman who washed and anointed his feet (Lk 7:36–50), and his dialogue with the Samaritan woman at the well. (Jn 4:1–42)

[2] Pope Benedict XVI, *Jesus of Nazareth Part II: Holy Week* (London: Catholic Truth Society, 2011), pp. 171–172.

Chapter Four

Humiliated

You shall not curse the deaf or put a stumbling block before the blind… (Lv 19:14)

The humiliations associated with being incapacitated are many and various, and can be worse than physical pain and discomfort. They often stem from the attitudes and responses of others. Whereas the trials of life, common to all, can be surmounted with humour and perseverance, humiliations carelessly inflicted on us when we are already suffering are not so easy to shrug off. We may experience people's lack of understanding about our illness or disability, a lack of understanding reflected in media focus on people pretending to be disabled or sick in order to receive sympathy or social benefits. Sometimes able-bodied people are chosen to play at being disabled to see what it is 'like', rather than listening to those who already know. Some dramas, rather than focussing on the real struggles of disabled people, portray disabled characters as ungraciously rebuffing attempts to help them.

Sick people are portrayed as refusing treatment. In reality, true pity is hard to come by, and it is more usual for patients to be refused treatment than to refuse it.[1] Chronic sickness is sometimes seen by secular society as a failure of mental attitude, and by the religious, as a failure of faith. All this adds insult to injury.

In the face of humiliation and lack of understanding it is tempting to comfort our selves. In the absence of true pity, it is tempting to avoid those who don't help, or become frustrated by inappropriate attempts to help.

And those who passed by derided him, shaking their heads, and saying, 'Aha! You who would destroy the temple and build it in three days, save yourself, and come down from the cross!' (Mk 15:29–30)

After being arrested, interrogated and scourged, Jesus, an innocent man, was beaten up by the Roman soldiers for their amusement; they 'plaited a crown of thorns, and put it on his head, and clothed him in a purple robe; they came up to him, saying, "Hail, King of the Jews!" and struck him with their hands' (Jn 19:1–3). Pilate had Jesus, still wearing the crown of thorns and the purple robe, brought out before the crowd, but despite the good He had done, He was rejected (Jn 19:4–7).[2] The same happened when He was 'lifted up' on the cross: He was derided rather than helped, despite the unstinting help He had given to others. Then, as now, those in positions of power, both high and low, used that power to do evil rather than good.

Our Lord allowed Himself to be humiliated for our sakes, just as He humbled Himself to be born in a stable. To Pilate's demand, 'Where are you from?'

Jesus made no reply (Jn 19:8–9). To give a true answer to the Roman governor's question about his origins would have forced the issue; instead, Jesus allowed all the key players in the Passion drama, including those who abused Him, the dignity of free will; He put the truth before them, but they chose to reject it. He showed them His true identity; but they were not expecting to see the face of God covered in bruises, blood and spittle.

A Healing Ministry

Confronted by a woman who had been bent double for eighteen years, Jesus laid hands on her and healed her. The healing took place in a synagogue, whose president, anxious to defend the Law, protested that Jesus had healed on the Sabbath. Using the rabbinical 'how much more' argument, Jesus, rather than condemning the care of animals, built on that argument an even greater case for caring for human beings: 'Does not each one of you on the Sabbath untie his ox or his donkey from the manger, and lead it away to water it?' (Lk 13:10–17). The use of physical means of healing was classed as work, but healing was God's work, thus Jesus was making a statement about His own identity. The attitude of valuing animals more than people is by no means a thing of the past.[3] Then, as now, the disabled were often treated as less important than the able-bodied, and were kept at the margins of society.[4] On another occasion, a disabled man was humiliated by being treated as a nuisance and an interruption to normal life: the crowd that followed Jesus to Jericho objected to the shouts of a blind man, Bartimaeus, who called out, 'Son of David, Jesus, have pity on me!' He may even have interrupted a discourse on the subject of charity, but the crowd, annoyed, told him to be quiet. Socially as well as physically Bartimaeus had fallen behind—he had 'fallen out of the loop'; life went on, leaving him by the wayside. Undeterred, Bartimaeus called all the louder and was at last brought forward. Jesus asked the man good-humouredly: 'What do you want me to do for you?' (Mark 10:46–52). As with the healing of the woman with the haemorrhage, Jesus pitied rather than patronised, seeing the man as a human being with free will rather than a 'case' to be 'dealt with'. Rather than viewing Bartimaeus as an irritating interruption to His work Jesus showed, by interrupting His progress, that healing Bartimaeus was His work; it was God's work.

Deep in thy wounds, Lord, hide and shelter me...[5]

In those days – and still, in many parts of the world—the incapacitated relied for help on their families and on charity. Like Bartimaeus many begged for a living. The best places to beg were by the side of a well-travelled road and in busy towns; small wonder that there are many Gospel stories of Jesus healing disabled people 'along the way'. The best place of all was at the Temple. Along with fasting and prayer, the giving of alms to the needy was one of the pillars of the Jewish religion, and the Temple attracted great crowds of pious pilgrims going to fulfil a vow, to pray, to give thanks, make atonement, or offer sacrifice. Although the noise of a large crowd alerted beggars to the approach of potential alms-givers, it also made it difficult for their requests to be heard; already humiliated by having to beg, the beggars' hearts were hardened as they competed to attract attention, bellowing all the louder to extract money from passers-by whose hearts had become hardened to their plight. Bartimaeus was one such claimant. Rather than rebuking his clamour, however, Jesus addressed his needs. Jesus had seen the bent-over woman, and the woman with the haemorrhage, huddled in the margins of society, and placed them in the centre. He did not, however, overlook the effects of sin on the spirit: when a paralysed man was lowered by his friends through the roof of a house where He was teaching, in hope of a cure, Jesus forgave the man's sins before healing him physically (Lk 5:17–26). Similarly, at the Pool of Bethzatha in Jerusalem, after healing a man who had been paralysed for thirty-eight years—he had no friends to help him into the Pool, where it was believed that the first person to get into the water when the surface moved would be healed—Jesus warned, 'Sin no more, that nothing worse befall you' (Jn 5:1–14).

Jesus was not referring to the belief that disability was the result of sin, either of the disabled person, or, in the case of those born disabled, the parents. He taught the same regarding other misfortunes, as with the fate of the Galileans who were offering sacrifice when they were killed by Pilate (Lk 13:1–5). Our Lord's approach was radically different from that of humanity's, as seen most clearly in the healing of the blind man at the Temple, when the man's disability was blamed on the sins of his parents (Jn 9:27–34). Such attitudes persist to this day in secular form. Today, illness is often blamed on unhealthy lifestyles, and lack of healing is blamed on the lack of a positive attitude on the part of sufferers. Some parents of disabled children, blamed for not choosing abortion, are held responsible for their children's plight.[6] Blaming the victim absolves the rest of society from the duty of care, but adds a burden of humiliation to the suffering of the victim.

Healing Balm from the Church

In His parables Jesus taught that only the humble will be able to enter the Kingdom of Heaven; but also that the Kingdom of Heaven is not what people think it is; it will not 'arrive' in a specific place, with a great fanfare. The Kingdom, Jesus said, was amongst us – actually within us (Lk 17:20–21). It is to be found in the humblest position—the lowest seat at the feast; the place that nobody wants (Lk 14:8). Everyone wants to be strong; nobody wants to be weak and vulnerable; but Jesus, setting a child among His followers, said: 'Truly, I say unto you, unless you turn and become like children, you will never enter the kingdom of heaven. Whoever humbles himself like this child, he is the greatest in the kingdom of heaven' (Mt 18:3–4). Children are humble and trusting, and the Kingdom of Heaven is to be found in humility, because that is where God is. We must have the humility to trust in God, who in His humility entrusted Himself to us in the form of a little child.

In His humility Jesus allowed Himself to be humiliated. When we suffer humiliation, it is easy to fall into the Devil's trap—to become spiritually paralysed. When we are hurting, it is hard to pity others. It is easier to avoid those who ignore us or offer inappropriate help—but in so doing we also avoid the opportunity to help them. In the Sacrament of Reconciliation we can confess the times we have humiliated others, or ignored their humiliation. We can feel Christ's pity flowing from His wounds, cleansing and healing us.

Through us, His pity can flow over all those whom we meet on our journey.

> *Forgive us our trespasses, as we forgive those who trespass against us… (Mt 6:12)*

Jesus was blameless; His treatment at the hands of the soldiers and those who passed by at His crucifixion added humiliation to injustice. His whole life had been sacrificed to the good of the world, which repaid Him with rejection. Still His pity flowed like the blood from His wounds; even after death, from the wound of the cruel spear, pity flowed in the water gushing from His side. His weakness tempted men to humiliate Him, but in suffering their humiliations willingly His love proved to be stronger than their hate. In the Eucharist Jesus strengthens us with His body and blood to face daily humiliation for the sake of truly living and truly loving.

> *Thanks be to Jesus for suffering humiliation for my sake.*

Pray for enemies. Pray that our world will not succumb to the temptation to do away with pity, hardening its heart against the needy—like the Spartans who exposed their disabled infants to the cruel elements, or the tribes who sacrificed their babies and their old people. Pray that governments and peoples will oppose abortion and euthanasia. Pray for disabled people who in many parts of the world are forced to beg for a living; for the needy everywhere who experience humiliation; that they may have the courage to ask for the help they need. Pray for prisoners, that they may be humanely treated. When humiliation threatens to harden our hearts, the Divine Mercy chain of contemplative prayer can help:[7] 'For the sake of His sorrowful passion, have mercy on us, and on the whole world'.

Lord of all pity, I praise you.

Ask St Veronica, who wiped the face of Christ on His way to Calvary, commemorated in the Stations of the Cross, that we may be moved by true pity—not lip service, but a willingness to find out the real needs of the needy. Pray that even if we can only help a little, we will offer that help rather than passing by on the other side (Lk 10:31–32). Ask the women of Jerusalem, who mourned for Jesus on His way to the Cross (Lk 23:26–32) to help us show pity for those condemned to death by execution, genocide, euthanasia, and abortion. Pray to Our Lady of Lourdes to help all those visiting her Shrine; for all those who cannot go on pilgrimage—who have 'no one to help them into the healing waters'—that healing miracles will relieve suffering and strengthen faith.[8]

You anoint my head with oil... (Ps 23)

Come to me, all who labour and are heavy laden, and I will give you rest. (Mt 11:28)

Notes

[1] In a landmark legal judgement, the Tony Bland case (1993) redefined artificially delivered nutrition and hydration as medical treatment; this decision allowed for Mr Bland, who suffered brain trauma as a result of the Hillsborough football ground disaster in 1990 and was deemed to have no prospect of recovery, to have his artificial feeding tubes removed, leading to his death. The Mental Incapacity Act (2005) gave legal sanction to patient decisions to refuse treatment, which as a consequence of the Bland case included artificial feeding.

However, there is no legal imperative to respect the wishes of those who want to be treated, including artificial feeding: when a man suffering from a degenerative brain disease sought legal assurances that he would be artificially fed if he lost the ability to communicate, the Government argued that to guarantee the right of all patients to tube feeding in the event of their incapacity would be too costly; see: A. Farmer, *By Their Fruits: Eugenics, Population Control, and the Abortion Campaign* (Washington DC: Catholic University of America Press, 2008), pp. 262–263.

2   Pope Benedict XVI, *Jesus of Nazareth Part II: Holy Week* (London: Catholic Truth Society, 2011), pp. 186–188.

3   The Animals (Scientific Procedures) Act 1986 ensures protection in the 'foetal, larval or embryonic form' (Chapter 14, 1(2)) but the '"protected animal" for the purposes of this Act means any living vertebrate other than man' (Chapter 14, 1(1)) (London: The Stationery Office, 1986).

4   The Fertilisation and Embryology Act (1990) reduced the upper time limit for abortion from 28 to 24 weeks but exempted abortions for suspected disability, thus affected foetuses may be aborted up to birth (London: The Stationery Office, 1990).

5   Pope John XXII, Hymn, *Soul of My Saviour*.

6   See: A. Farmer, *By Their Fruits: Eugenics, Population Control, and the Abortion Campaign* (Washington DC: Catholic University of America Press, 2008), pp. 245–247.

7   See 'Prayers and Devotions', p. 113 below.

8   In 1858, near Lourdes in France, Our Lady appeared several times to a young peasant girl, Bernadette Soubirous, revealing to her a spring with healing powers; her Shrine became famous for its many cures; Our Lady also referred to herself as the Immaculate Conception. See *Catechism of the Catholic Church*, 491–492.

Chapter Five

Forsaken

My God, my God, why have you forsaken me?
(Ps 22; Mt 27:46–47; Mk 15:34)

After a lengthy illness, or a disability compounded by new health problems, with little hope of healing, we may feel spiritual as well as physical isolation. Like the lepers, and like Job, we may feel that we are being shunned. Like the woman with the haemorrhage, even in a crowd we can feel alone in the universe. We may even feel abandoned by God. Does He exist? If He does, has He forgotten me?

At such times we may experience feelings of pointlessness; alone in a spiritual desert, that arid place between the living and the dead, we feel we are 'just going through the motions'. The spectre of despair hovers over us, like the vultures hovering above the Cross.

I thirst. (Jn 19:28)

During His ministry Jesus frequently refreshed His spirit by going to a secluded place in order to be at one with His Father. (Lk 5:15–16) However, at the point of death He experienced a terrifying isolation. Suspended between earth and sky, the raucous shouts of soldiers and passers-by ringing in His ears, Jesus more than ever needed to be alone with God—Father and Son, persons distinct but the same, united in will. Now He was to fully share the final human experience, death—not eased by seeking His Father's help, or by His own supernatural powers, but experienced as a man—like all men. However, even at the very end Jesus did not despair.

Father, into your hands I commit my spirit. (Lk 23:46)

In His ministry Jesus used His healing powers to defeat this implacable enemy of humanity many times. He had even snatched His friend Lazarus, as well as the daughter of Jairus (Mk 5:22–43) and the widow's son at Nain (Lk 7:11–17) from the very jaws of death. However, on Calvary, it seemed that death would finally triumph, as Jesus was laid, cold and alone in a borrowed tomb. His greatest miracle of all—the death of death—was witnessed only by the angels, but on that first Easter Sunday He was no ghost. His resurrected body was real, although capable of changing in appearance as He willed it. When Mary Magdalen encountered Jesus, she thought Him a gardener. On recognising His voice she was told: 'Do not hold me, for I have not yet ascended to the Father...' (Jn 20:11–18) He passed through locked doors (Jn 20:19–21) and was seen by the Disciples in two places at once—on the road to Emmaus, and in Jerusalem (Lk 24:13–35). On the latter occasion He said 'handle me, and see; for a spirit has not flesh and bones as you see that I have'.

He asked if they had anything to eat; they 'gave him a piece of broiled fish, and he took it and ate before them' (Lk 24:36–43). There were to be many more appearances before Jesus ascended into Heaven. Many continue to dispute the Resurrection, but not even the Roman authorities or the Temple party, who would be most anxious to scotch the rumours, could produce a corpse.

> *Even though I walk through the valley of the shadow of death, I fear no evil; for you are with me... (Ps 23)*

We are familiar—perhaps too familiar—with the story of the Resurrection; it is understandable that the Disciples, despite our Lord's careful preparation for His passion and its aftermath, did not instantly recognise the risen Christ. Moreover, despite His warnings about the nature of His Kingdom, it was difficult for them to abandon hopes of a glorious Messiah who would vanquish the occupying Roman army and bestow positions of privilege and power on His friends—even when those hopes had been finally dashed on a hill outside Jerusalem, between two thieves. Such a humiliating end to the Master's story was not what the Disciples had in mind; they had envisaged triumph, not suffering. Nevertheless, Jesus was patient with the doubts of St Thomas, who was not present when He appeared to the others; but He also said:

> *Blessed are those who have not seen and yet believe. (Jn 20:19–29)*

We may never understand, in this life at least, the purpose of suffering and the reason why bad things happen to good people; if we did, we would know as much as God Himself. Like Job all we can do is remain quiet before God, just as God stands silent before our accusations; just as Jesus stood mute before Pilate, refusing to defend Himself, 'like a lamb that is led to the slaughter, and like a sheep that before its shearers is silent' (Is 53:7). The purpose of Our Lord's suffering was to bring us salvation; we know that God brings good out of evil; and we know that He requires our co-operation. The parable of the talents (Mt 25:14–30) reminds us that God will call us to account for what we have done with our lives, including what we have done with the suffering we have experienced. Few of us, unprompted, would see suffering as a gift, but the Church teaches that it too can be seen as a treasure that can be multiplied, for good or evil – the choice is ours.

Healing Balm from the Church

The medieval devotion to the Five Wounds emphasised the comfort that Christ's Wounds could offer the dying in their final moments; famous penitents like St Peter, St Mary Magdalen and Dismas the Good Thief were cited to dispel feelings of despair.[1] When we are tempted to give way to such feelings we are in most urgent need of reconciliation with God; we need to be healed of our spiritual isolation in the Sacrament that allows us to experience the death of sin and the resurrection of hope.

> *And lead us not into temptation, but deliver us from evil. (Mt 6:13)*

Jesus told the Disciples: 'Truly, truly, I say to you, unless you eat the flesh of the Son of man and drink his blood, you have no life in you; he who eats my flesh and drinks my blood has eternal life, and I will raise him up at the last day' (Jn 6:53–54). At His final Passover he gave them bread and wine, saying, 'Do this in remembrance of me' (Lk 22:19–20). At His Ascension into Heaven He told them: 'Behold, I am with you always, to the close of the age' (Mt 28:20). In the Eucharist, Our Lord keeps His pledges, giving us His body, blood, soul, and divinity; the gift of everlasting life. Jesus, who felt our despair, can resurrect our hope out of His suffering. When we experience dryness of spirit, He holds out the cup of living water: 'Whoever drinks of the water that I shall give him will never thirst...' (Jn 4:14).

Thanks be to Jesus for the Resurrection, the ultimate triumph over despair.

Pray for strangers. Pray that we may not be afraid to get closer to God; that we may not give in to despair. Pray that good may come out of evil. Before the crucifix we can pour out our problems; nothing is too bad, or too big—or too small—to leave at the foot of the Cross.

Lord of all hope, I praise you.

Pray for the thousands of people, including children, who are imprisoned around the world, as well as those 'imprisoned' by physical or psychological problems; show them that they have not been abandoned. Offer up feelings of failure, hopelessness and anxiety for those tempted to give in to the ultimate despair, that they may know there is hope. Ask the help of St Rita of Cascia, patron of the helpless. Pray the Novena of St Jude, patron saint of hopeless causes, for suicides. Ask St John, who stood at the foot of the Cross, for the courage to stand by others in their trials; ask Our Lady, who had the courage to share her only Son's pain, humiliation and apparent failure (Jn 19:26–27), to watch and pray for us in our hour of need; to share with us, in death, the sure and certain hope of the Resurrection; as she was conceived without sin,[2] to help us to confront our own sins and forgive the sins of others.

> *For I am sure that neither death, nor life, nor angels, nor principalities, nor things present, nor things to come, nor powers, nor height, nor depth, nor anything else in all creation, will be able to separate us from the love of God in Christ Jesus our Lord. (Rm 8:38–39)*
>
> *I am the resurrection and the life; he who believes in me, though he die, yet shall he live, and whoever lives and believes in me shall never die. (Jn 11:26)*
>
> *My cup overflows. (Ps 23)*

Notes

[1] E. Duffy, *The Stripping of the Altars: Traditional Religion in England c.1400–c.1580* (New Haven and London: Yale University Press, 1992), pp. 241–242.

[2] *Catechism of the Catholic Church*, 490–494.

Conclusion

Balm for a Wounded Spirit

Restore to me the joy of your salvation, and uphold me with a willing spirit. (Ps 51)

It is a normal human response to seek quick and easy solutions to the problem of suffering; to want to get back to the Garden of Eden. If each of us has a cross to bear, we would rather lay down that cross. In another garden, the garden of Gethsemane, Jesus prayed to do just that: 'Father, if you are willing, remove this chalice from me…' In the mystery of the Trinity, Jesus wrestled with His Father's will, but concluded: 'Not my will, but yours, be done' (Lk 22:42). In the Prayer that Our Lord taught us we say 'deliver us from evil'. We may be able to avoid some evils, but it seems that some of us cannot lay down the cross of sickness.

Our Lord's healing miracles teach us that we do right to seek help. However, in Jesus we see the unavoidable human problems of betrayal, loss of identity, injustice, humiliation, and isolation, confronted by Him as a human being; how He overcame them, even to vanquishing humanity's greatest problem, death.

> *You will be sorrowful, but your sorrow will turn into joy. (Jn 16:20)*

Jesus did not say that His followers would be immune to suffering—rather the reverse! He said 'If any man would come after me, let him deny himself and take up his cross and follow me' (Mt 16:24). Indeed, 'He who does not take his cross and follow me is not worthy of me' (Mt 10:38). Suffering for the sake of following Christ is a daily reality for Christians in some parts of the world.[1] However, He also said 'My yoke is easy, and my burden is light' (Mt 11:28–30). Jesus helps us carry our cross—in His word, in His sacraments, in His Holy Spirit, and in the living Church He founded, of which He pledged 'the powers of death shall not prevail against it' (Mt 16:16–19).

> *If this is how You treat Your friends... Well, then, no wonder You have so few of them! (St Teresa of Avila)*

Though we ponder the mystery of evil, suffering and injustice, the greatest mystery of all is why God's help, so freely offered to humanity, is ignored or rejected. Perhaps the key to this mystery is to be found in humanity's other, equally enduring, problems—forgetfulness and fear. God provided an answer to the first of these when He instituted the Passover to remind His Chosen People of how He rescued them from enslavement in Egypt (Ex 12:15–20). It was at one particular Passover meal in Jerusalem that the Son of God instituted the Eucharist, the new Covenant: 'Do this in remembrance of me' (Lk 22:19–20). For humanity's other great problem, St John tells us that 'God is love' (1 Jn 4:8). Since Jesus and the Father 'are one' (Jn 10:30) Jesus is perfect love, stronger than fear—even fear of death.

Perfect love casts out fear. (1 Jn 4:18)

Death, the final injustice, did not strike the final blow in the cosmic battle; sin could not kill God, but we can allow sin to kill our hope in God. We have been created free—free to choose how we respond to the crosses we do not want but must bear; to embrace them freely, or allow them to drag us down into the dirt of sin and death. We know that God will never leave us, and will suffer—is suffering—with us. We can betray God a thousand times a day but He will never betray us. If He can forgive us, then surely we can forgive ourselves and each other.

A man once gave a great banquet, and invited many; and at the time for the banquet he sent his servant to say to those who had been invited, 'Come; for all is now ready.' (Lk 14:16–17)

Only Christ, who suffered the five physical wounds for our sakes, can see our spiritual wounds; only Christ, wonderful counsellor, perfect physician, Prince of Peace, can heal them, through His words, His Holy Spirit, His Sacraments, His Church. The Church He founded is not a collection of buildings, or a nebulous idea, but a living thing.

This is my commandment, that you love one another as I have loved you. (Jn 15:12)

The English mystic Mother Julian of Norwich, in her tenth revelation, saw the Wound in Christ's side, and proclaimed it a beautiful place: it allowed access to His heart, and was large enough for all humanity to rest in peace and love. However, the Wounds of Christ are not a final resting place in this world: our parched spirits quenched with His saving grace, we must share this grace with the world.[2] The love of Jesus is not a vague cosy feeling to be hoarded, but a treasure to be shared. His words are not just words but a call to ministry: 'Greater love has no man than this, that a man lay down his life for his friends' (Jn 15:12–13). In recognising Christ's wounds we see more clearly the invisible wounds that each one of us bears; thus we can 'Encourage the faint-hearted, help the weak, be patient with them all' (1 Th 5:14). The communion of saints, growing day by day, provides an abundant harvest of helpers for the helpless. The Church, from her treasure house of riches, provides encouragement for us to celebrate, to thank God for all that we are and all that we can do, together with the hope that, though crucified with Christ, we may be resurrected with Him. We may feel that we do not know where we are going, but when we look back in faith we see that He has guided us every step of the way—even through the dark valley.

Surely goodness and mercy shall follow me all the days of my life...(Ps 23)

When we are in good health and good spirits, we may not feel an urgent need for the Sacrament of Reconciliation; it seems a cruel twist of fate that when we need it most we are unable to participate in it so easily. Nevertheless, the blessings are out of all proportion to the effort involved, clearing the obstacles that stand in the way of fully receiving Jesus into our lives. He illustrated this mystery in His parable about the man who issued invitations to a banquet only to have them rejected; those invited 'all alike made excuses'. The truth was that they did not need what He had to offer; they simply were not hungry enough (Lk 14:12–24). This is the mystery, and the beauty, of suffering: that it makes us hungry for God, just as He hungers for us to return His love. When we offer up our sufferings to Him we find ourselves becoming more like the One who offered His sufferings for the world. When we accept the invitation to join our sufferings to His, we find we have accepted His invitation to that joyful banquet, at which God Himself is the food: truly our Host. Will we have the courage to give our bodies, with all their infirmities, up to Him, as He gave His body for us? For if we claim a share in the sufferings of the Lamb of God we will also share in the joy of the Banquet of the Lamb.

So often we would choose to by-pass Good Friday and go straight to Easter Sunday; to by-pass the Crucifixion and go straight to the triumph of the Resurrection; but if we refuse to recognise the suffering Christ, how will we recognise the Risen Christ? At the Annunciation Our Lady, 'the handmaid of the Lord', had the courage to say 'yes' to God (Lk 26–38); at Cana she had the courage to say 'yes' to her Son's public ministry, knowing where it would lead (Jn 2:1–11); but trusting that it would lead beyond the Crucifixion, to that joyful feast in the Kingdom of Heaven. As our Lady co-operated in our Redemption,[3] ask her help for the courage to say 'yes' to suffering in order to claim that redemption.

You prepare a table before me in the presence of my enemies... I shall dwell in the house of the Lord for ever. (Ps 23)

Notes

1. See: *Persecuted and Forgotten? A Report on Christians oppressed for their Faith, 2011 Edition* (Sutton, Surrey: Aid to the Church in Need, 2011).
2. E. Duffy, *The Stripping of the Altars: Traditional Religion in England c.1400 — c.1580* (New Haven and London: Yale University Press, 1992), p. 244.
3. According to St Irenaeus, 'Being obedient she became the cause of salvation for herself and for the whole human race'. See *Adversus haereses*, 3, 22, 4 in J. P. Migne, *Patrologia graeca*, 7/1, 959A, as cited in *Catechism of the Catholic Church*, 494.

Addendum

A Word on Suicide

Increasingly, 'assisted suicide' is presented as the answer to human suffering—even demanded as a human right. The temptation to control the time and manner of our dying seems to offer the prospect of controlling the last, most mysterious, yet most certain problem in life. It offers the prospect of healing the wounds inflicted on our souls through the betrayals, humiliations and injustices of life.

However, the only effective answer to human suffering is love; in committing suicide we would curtail our capacity to love and be loved; we would be inflicting a fatal wound on an already wounded spirit. The 'death as a solution' approach is based on the assumption that the earthly life is the only life. As such, it offers an easy way out of suffering, a promise of true rest, eternal sleep—but in this life we only know we have had a good night's sleep when we wake up. Death without God would not mean eternal sleep; it would mean eternity without love. As created beings we cannot be uncreated. If we deny God's saving power by grasping at our own deaths, it is more certain that we will awake from earthly sleep to eternal wakefulness; to eternal separation from the love of Christ and His mercy; for we are the only ones who can sever the tie of love.

In a materialistic society it is difficult to defend suffering as a positive thing; even if we are confident in making such claims, they may be dismissed with the accusation that we should not attempt to control the choices other people want to make. Indeed, it is impossible to comprehend all the suffering in the world, much of it endured by good people. But God hears every cry. Those who live in Western nations are spared much of the day-to-day privations of developing countries, but sometimes God stands aside and allows us to suffer a mere hint of the bitter wind that blows through the lives of the poor. He allows us to see a mere fraction of the misery that He sees. C. S. Lewis wrote eloquently about suffering, but it was only when his wife was dying of cancer that he was able to speak with true authority on the subject.[1]

The sick and disabled are the most eloquent defenders of the right to life of the vulnerable, because we speak from a position of vulnerability. No one can accuse us of heartlessly laying down rules for others that do not affect us. Although we hope for healing, and continue to seek it, we can draw upon our experience of suffering to help others in the fight to stay alive until natural death. This demands more courage than committing suicide because it demands our trust in God; but wherever the journey takes us, God has been there first—even when we feel abandoned. Jesus, on the cross, experienced the whole process of death for our sakes. However, in Gethsemane He prayed to be spared His fate—to accomplish God's will, but in another way; (Lk 22:42) thus we need have no qualms in asking God to 'let the cup of suffering pass' but, like Jesus, to accept the suffering if that is the only way God's will can be accomplished. He doesn't want us to suffer, but when we do, He wants us to bring it to Him so that He can comfort us.

St Thérèse of Lisieux, the 'Little Flower', lost her mother when she was very young, but through that experience gave us the beautiful picture of God bending down to pick us up when we are unable to do anything for ourselves. When we suffer, like little children we can become angry with God, because we can rationalise suffering with our heads, but not with our hearts. We'll probably never be able to 'explain' suffering to the satisfaction of our emotions; however, paradoxically, the idea of the redemptive value of suffering, under which we are helping God to redeem the world, makes sense to the heart even when it doesn't to the head.

If, in the drive to abolish suffering we abolish the idea of God, our whole moral cosmos becomes meaningless, because only God gives meaning to the world and thus to suffering. Those who have tried to abolish the idea of good and evil have been left with no God to help them conquer the evil, because good and evil are more than mere ideas: they are objective realities. If there is no God, morality becomes whatever we want it to be; life has no meaning, and no intrinsic value. If we abolish the idea of caring as a response to suffering because it does not abolish the suffering, we are left with killing as the only solution to suffering; then, suicide becomes 'assisted suicide', which swiftly becomes euthanasia. The suicide campaign would get rid of suffering by getting rid of the sufferer. Take away Mother Teresa and we are left with the State 'euthanasor' armed with a lethal hypodermic.

The Church teaches that suicide offends against God, who entrusted life to our stewardship rather than our ownership. It offends against the love of self, the love of neighbour and the love of human society. God commanded us, 'You shall love your neighbour as yourself'; (Lv 19:18) if we demand the 'right' to kill our selves, can we, in conscience, withhold such a right from our neighbour? Suicide is more than a simple personal choice. Many suicide attempts are the result of depression; they are often cries for help; many foiled suicides are grateful for having been frustrated; for being given the opportunity to change their minds.[2]

The Church teaches that we should pray for suicides and that we should not despair of God's mercy upon them; but neither should we gamble our immortal souls on the presumption that we will get into the Kingdom of Heaven by the broad easy path rather than the narrow gateway. It should console sufferers to know that their earthly suffering, if they offer it up to God, is akin to that preparation for Heaven that takes place in Purgatory. In a very real sense they have already met the suffering Christ on the road to Calvary and helped Him carry His burden, the sins of the world. However, night can bring the deepest loneliness to those who suffer, especially those who endure sleeplessness, depression, pain as well as other symptoms that are difficult to control. At such times, unlike during the day, there is little to distract us from temptations and unwelcome thoughts.

The English devotion to the Five Wounds inspired tales of Christ appearing to the sick to urge their repentance before the Judgement;[3] they were only too aware how easily we can swing between the sins of presumption and despair when confronting the awful mystery of death. When such temptations come, when human help is far away, we do not have to suffer alone, for God is always there. Indeed, it is those times when there is no human help available, when we have to rely utterly on Him, that we feel His love most. He will never be asleep, too busy, or 'not around' when we call, and will surely direct us to resources that give us hope. When Jesus was tempted in the desert, angels were sent to comfort Him (Mt 4:11). God gave each of us a guardian angel (Mt 18:10) to whom we can appeal for help at such moments.

At times of extreme stress God can feel far away; in the face of His greatness we can feel very small and unimportant. Sometimes we feel afraid that by 'not putting up with things' we are showing a lack of faith. We may feel guilty at approaching Jesus in prayer yet again, when we know so many people are worse off than ourselves. We may simply feel tired of struggling to swim against the tide of hopelessness. At such times, Our Lady, who intercedes for the sick,[4] will quietly take our pleas to her Son on our behalf. If we feel we cannot trust ourselves not to sin, we can entrust our safety and spiritual wellbeing to the Mother of God — Mary of Nazareth, Mother of all, who will watch over us as lovingly as she watched over the Child Jesus in her arms.[5]

If we humbly ask the Holy Spirit to come into our hearts, and clear our minds of all thought, we will feel His breath upon us, strengthening us against temptation; that we may be delivered from evil. He will help us remember that whatever the world and the Devil teaches — that suffering is useless and those who suffer are 'better off out of it' — God loves us and cherishes every atom of our being, not for what we can do, but for who we are — His children. This truth is anathema to Satan, who tempts us with heavenly visions of eternal peace in the hope that we will spend eternity in Hell with him; the quickest and most effective way to banish the temptation to suicide is to offer up such thoughts to the glory of God.

It may seem strange to mention joy and suffering in the same sentence, but when suffering is embraced for the sake of the Kingdom we find joy in the most unexpected places. Our Lady experienced the double-edged sword of joy and sorrow, as it was foretold when she presented the Child Jesus at the Temple: (Lk 2:22–35) as she joyfully cradled her infant Son, she would sorrowfully cradle His broken body after He was taken down from the Cross. In G. K. Chesterton's *Ballad of the White Horse* Our Lady asks King Alfred, facing the threat of the Danes, 'Do you have joy without a cause, Yea, faith without a hope?'[6] Chesterton, who suffered deep depression in his youth — whose brother-in-law committed suicide —[7] saw joy as a kind of aperture into God's infinite realm, a response to simply being; joy is Heaven breaking into our material world,[8] as when the angel host split the sky over Bethlehem with joyful song on the night Christ was born (Lk 2:13–14).

When everything is black as black, suddenly a tree, a flower, or just a blade of grass seems to be bursting with praise for its Creator. I once asked to see some birds in the garden — a rare event since I am unable to put out special food for them — and promised that if He would send some I wouldn't put it down to coincidence; the next minute He sent a great flock!

Often He sends such surprises when we don't ask, at just the time when we need them. It could be argued that I simply happen to be looking for them at times of particular need; but they always take me by surprise. On such occasions they are the gifts that we do not even know we need until we receive them. God knows our suffering, and He knows what we need (Mt 6:8). It is as if He is saying, 'Not yet; but I have not forgotten you'.

These shafts of joy amid suffering remind us of St John of the Cross and his 'dark night of the soul' — the darkness that can afflict those who have every material luxury. The darkness is a sign that we have excluded God from our lives; it is evidence of the soul's existence, and thus of God's existence. So is joy in the midst of suffering. Unlike happiness, joy is not transient and dependent on good health or good fortune. It differs according to individual circumstances, but is eternal and always from the same source: the fount of pure joy that springs from the Wounds of Christ, those never-failing wells of grace, pity, mercy, and everlasting life.

> *I call heaven and earth to witness against you this day, that I have set before you life and death, blessing and curse; therefore choose life, that you and your descendants may live... (Dt 30:19)*

> *I am the resurrection and the life, and whoever lives and believes in me shall never die. (Mt 11:25)*

Notes

1. C. S. Lewis, *The Problem of Pain* (London: Centenary Press, 1940); Idem, *A Grief Observed* (London: Faber & Faber, 1961).
2. Alison Davis, national co-ordinator of the SPUC group *No Less Human*, who has several serious, painful, and incurable disabling conditions, has often spoken of her relief and gratitude that helping someone to commit suicide has not been made legal in this country, since her attempts at suicide, made during a lengthy period of depression, were foiled by friends and medical staff; had she succeeded in her attempts, she would not have experienced the best and most productive periods of her life.
3. E. Duffy, *The Stripping of the Altars: Traditional Religion in England c.1400–c.1580* (New Haven and London: Yale University Press: 1992), pp. 246–247.
4. See: *Litany of Our Lady of Lourdes* in 'Prayers and Devotions', pp. 105–107 below.
5. 'Jesus is Mary's only Son, but her spiritual motherhood extends to all men whom indeed he came to save' (*Catechism of the Catholic Church*, 501).
6. 'Night shall be thrice night over you,/ And heaven an iron cope./ Do you have joy without a cause,/ Yea, faith without a hope?' (G. K. Chesterton, "*The Ballad of the White Horse*" in *The Works of G. K. Chesterton* (Ware, Herts: Wordsworth Poetry Library, 1995), p. 173).
7. I. Ker, *G. K. Chesterton: A Biography* (Oxford: Oxford University Press, 2011), pp. 203–204.
8. A. Nichols, *G. K. Chesterton, Theologian* (London: Darton, Longman & Todd Ltd, 2009), pp. 107–109.

BIBLIOGRAPHY

MAIN WORKS

Aid to the Church in Need, *Persecuted and Forgotten? A Report on Christians oppressed for their Faith, 2011 Edition.* Sutton, Surrey: Aid to the Church in Need, 2011.

Alexander, M., *Medievalism: the Middle Ages in modern England.* London/New Haven, Conn: Yale University Press, 2007.

Allen, C., *The Human Christ.* Oxford: Lion Publishing, 1998.

Aquilina, M., Flaherty, R. J., *The How-To Book of Catholic Devotions.* Indiana: Our Sunday Visitor Inc., 2000.

Asquith, C., *Shadowplay: the Hidden Beliefs and Coded Politics of William Shakespeare.* New York: Public Affairs, 2005.

Avi-Yonah, M., *Ancient Scrolls.* Jerusalem: Palphot Ltd., 1994.

Bauckham, R. (Ed.), *The Gospels for All Christians.* Edinburgh: T & T Clark, 1998.

Benedict XVI, *Jesus of Nazareth.* London: Bloomsbury, 2007.

Benedict XVI, *Jesus of Nazareth Part II: Holy Week.* London: Catholic Truth Society, 2011.

Blacker, C. P., *Eugenics: Galton and After.* London: Gerald Duckworth, 1952.

Burleigh, M., *Death and Deliverance: 'Euthanasia' in Germany 1900-1945*. Cambridge: Cambridge University Press, 1994.

Caraman, P., *John Gerard: The Autobiography of an Elizabethan*. London: Longmans, Green and Co., 1951.

Caraman, P., *The Western Rising 1549: The Prayer Book Rebellion*. Tiverton, Devon: Westcountry Books, 1999.

Chadwick, O., *The Reformation*. London: Penguin, 1990.

Chesterton, G. K., *Charles Dickens*. London: Methuen & Co. Ltd., 1906/1913.

Chesterton, G. K., *The Ballad of the White Horse, The Works of G. K. Chesterton*. Ware, Herts: Wordsworth Poetry Library, 1995.

Chesterton, G. K., *Twelve Types*. Norfolk, VA: IHS Press, 1902/2003.

Chesterton, G. K., *The Victorian Age in Literature*. London: Williams and Norgate, 1913/1919.

Chesterton, G. K., *A Short History of England*. London: Chatto & Windus, 1917.

Chesterton, G. K., *The Catholic Church and Conversion*. San Francisco: Ignatius Press, 1926/2006.

Chesterton, G. K., *The Thing*. London: Sheed & Ward, 1929.

Cobbett, W., *A History of the Protestant Reformation in England and Ireland*. London: Catholic Publishing & Bookselling Company, Limited, n.d.

Crusemann, F., *The Torah: Theological and Sociological History of Old Testament Law*. Edinburgh: T & T Clark, 1996.

Darwin, C., *On the Origin of Species*. London: Murray, 1859.

Darwin, C., *The Descent of Man*. London: Murray, 1871.

Dickens, C., *Nicholas Nickleby*. Ware, Herts: Wordsworth Classics, 1838-39/2000.

Dickens, C., *The Old Curiosity Shop*. Ware, Herts: Wordsworth Classics, 1841/1995.

Dickens, C., *A Christmas Carol. Best Ghost Stories*. Ware, Herts: Wordsworth Classics, 1843/1997.

Dickens, C., *Dombey and Son*. Ware, Herts: Wordsworth Classics, 1846-48/2002.

Dickens, C., *Little Dorrit*. Ware, Herts: Wordsworth Classics, 1855-57/2002.

Dickens, C., *Our Mutual Friend*. Ware, Herts: Wordsworth Classics, 1864-65/2002.

Dickens, A. G., *The Age of Humanism and Reformation*. Milton Keynes, Bucks: Open University Press, 1977.

Dowley, T. (ed.), *Discovering the Bible: Archaeologists look at Scripture*. London: Marshall Pickering, 1986.

Duffy, E., *The Stripping of the Altars: Traditional Religion in England c.1400 – c.1580*. New Haven and London: Yale University Press, 1992.

Farmer, A., *By Their Fruits: Eugenics, Population Control, and the Abortion Campaign*. Washington DC: Catholic University of America Press, 2008.

Fishbane, M. A., *The Garments of Torah: Essays in Biblical Hermeneutics*. Bloomington, Ind.: Indiana University Press, 1989.

Goldstein, Rabbi D., *Jewish Ethics*. London: Jewish Information Service, 1980.

Griffiths, G. Talbot, *Population Problems of the Age of Malthus*. London: Frank Cass & Co. Ltd., 1926/1967.

Jacobs, L., *A Jewish Theology*. London: Darton, Longman & Todd, 1973.

John Paul II, *Salvifici Doloris*. 1984.

Ker, I., *G. K. Chesterton: A Biography*. Oxford: Oxford University Press, 2011.

Kevles, D. J., *In the Name of Eugenics: Genetics and the Uses of Human Heredity*. Cambridge, Mass./London: Harvard University Press, 1995.

Lewis, C. S., *The Problem of Pain*. London: Geoffrey Bles: the centenary press, 1940.

Lewis, C. S., *A Grief Observed*. London Faber & Faber, 1961.

Malthus, T. R., *An Essay on the Principle of Population as It Affects the Future Improvement of Society, with Remarks on the Speculations of Mr Godwin, M. Condorcet, and Other Writers*. London, 1798; available at: http://www.econlib.org/cgi-bin/, at 30 November, 2005.

Mathew, D., *Catholicism in England 1535-1935: Portrait of a Minority: its Culture and Tradition*. London: The Catholic Book Club, 1938.

McCarthy, J. P., *Hilaire Belloc: Edwardian Radical*. Indianapolis: Liberty Press, 1978.

McLaren, A., *Our Own Master Race: Eugenics in Canada 1885-1945*. Toronto: J. P. McClelland and Stewart, 1990.

Millard, A., *Discoveries from Bible Times*. Oxford: Lion Publishing, 1990.

Nichols, A., *G. K. Chesterton, Theologian*. London: Darton, Longman & Todd Ltd., 2009.

Norman, E. R., *Anti-Catholicism in Victorian England*. London: George Allen and Unwin Ltd., 1968.

Orchard, B., *The Evolution of the Gospels*. London: CTS Publishing, 1990.

The Persecution of the Catholic Church in the Third Reich: Facts and Documents. London: Burns Oates, 1940.

The Pontifical Biblical Commission, *The Jewish people and their Sacred Scriptures in the Christian Bible*. Vatican City: Libreria Editrice Vaticana, 2002.

Russell, D. S., *From Judaism to Early Church*. London: SCM Press Ltd., 1986.

Sandmel, S., *A Jewish View of Jesus*. London: Jewish Information Service, n.d.

Shakespeare, W., *William Shakespeare: the Complete Works*. London: Collins, 1970.

Soloway, S., *Demography and Degeneration: Eugenics and the Declining Birthrate in Twentieth-Century Britain*. Chapel Hill: University of North Carolina Press, 1995.

Sternberger, G., *Introduction to the Talmud and Midrash*. Edinburgh: T & T Clark, 1996.

Stone, D., *Breeding Superman: Nietzsche, Race and Eugenics in Edwardian and Interwar Britain*. Liverpool: Liverpool University Press, 2002.

Taylor, R., *How to Read a Church*. London: Rider, 2007.

Thoma, C., Wyschogrod, M. (eds.), *Understanding Scripture: Explorations of Jewish and Christian Traditions of Interpretation*. New York: Paulist Press, 1987.

Thompson, E. P., *The Making of the English Working Class*. Harmondsworth, Middx: Pelican Books, 1984.

Trombley, S., *The Right to Reproduce: A History of Coercive Sterilization*. London: Weidenfeld & Nicolson, 1988.

Uglow, J., *William Hogarth: A Life and a World*. London: Faber & Faber, 2002.

Warren, C. R., *The Concept of the Chosen People*. London: Jewish Information Service, 1980.

Werfel, F., *The Song of Bernadette*. London: Hamish Hamilton, 1942.

Wright, C., *Knowing Jesus through the Old Testament*. London: Marshall Pickering, 1992.

OTHER RESOURCES

The Holy Bible, Revised Standard Version: 2nd Catholic Edition. San Francisco: Ignatius Press, 2006.

The New Jerusalem Bible. London: Darton, Longman & Todd, 1994.

Catechism of the Catholic Church. London: Geoffrey Chapman, 1995.

Catholic Prayer Book. Dublin: Dominican Publications, 1991.

Allegri, R., *Padre Pio: Man of Hope.* Atlanta, GA: Charis Books, 2000.

Axelrod, C., *And the Journey Begins.* Coleford, Gloucs.: Douglas McLean Paperback, 2005. Fr. Axelrod, the Church's only deafblind priest, ministers to deafblind people from the Diocese of Westminster, London.

Benedict XVI, *Way of the Cross.* London: Continuum, 2006.

Buckley, M., *Stories that Heal.* London: Darton, Longman & Todd, 1994.

Davis, A., *From Where I Sit: Living with Disability in an Able bodied World.* London: Triangle, 1989.

Dove, Fr. J., *Strange Vagabond of God: Memoir of John Bradburne.* Leominster, Herefordshire: Gracewing, 1997. John Bradburne, a lay Franciscan and talented poet, served as warden of a leper community in Zimbabwe, where he was murdered in 1979.

Foley, M. P., *Why do Catholics Eat Fish on Friday?* Basingstoke, Hants: Palgrave Macmillan, 2006.

Griffiths, A., *A Basic Catholic Dictionary.* Norwich: Canterbury Press, 2003.

Groeschel, Fr. B., von Hildebrand, Dr. A., *Suffering and what to do with it* (DVD). Ewtn, 2008.

Hahn, S., *Hail, Holy Queen: The Mother of God in the Word of God.* London: Darton, Longman & Todd, 2001.

Hardon, J. A., *With Us Today: On the Real Presence of Jesus Christ in the Eucharist.* Ypsilanti, MI: Veritas Press, 2003.

Holden, M. (Ed.), *Saints of the English Calendar.* Oxford: Family Publications, 2004.

John Paul II, *Be Not Afraid: Words of Faith, Hope and Love.* Philadelphia, PA: Courage Books, 2006.

Lewis, C. S., *The Screwtape Letters: Letters from a Senior to a Junior Devil.*

Manton, K., Muir, L., *The Gift of Julian of Norwich.* Mulgrave, Australia: John Garratt Publishing, 2005.

McGrath, A. E., *Christian Theology: an Introduction.* Oxford: Blackwell Publishers Ltd., 1994.

Mullen, P., *Shrines of Our Lady: A guide to fifty of the world's most famous Marian shrines.* London: Piatkus, 1998.

The Song of Bernadette (film), 1943.

Stone, E. Murray, Kelley, P., *Mother Teresa: A Life of Love.* Mahwah, NJ: Paulist Press, 1999.

Spink, K., *The Miracle, The Message, The Story: Jean Vanier and L'Arche.* London: Darton, Longman & Todd, 2006. Jean Vanier pioneered communities of able bodied and disabled people.

St Teresa of Avila, *Selections from the Interior Castle* (trans. and ed. E. Allison Peers). London: HarperCollins Spiritual Classics, 2004.

A Thérèse of Lisieux Prayer Book. Oxford: Family Publications, 2008.

Wendell, S., *The Rejected Body.* Oxford: Routledge, 1996.

USEFUL ORGANISATIONS

ALERT (against euthanasia): 27 Walpole Street, London SW3 4QS. Website: www.alertuk.org.

LIFE: Life House, Newbold Terrace, Leamington Spa, Warwicks CV32 4EA. Website: www.lifecharity.org.uk.

Human Life International: P.O. Box 4771, London, SE9 4XA. Website: www.hli.org.

Society for the Protection of Unborn Children (SPUC): Phyllis Bowman House, 5–6 St Matthew Street, Westminster, SW1P 2JT. SPUC's 'No Less Human' group champions the right to life of all disabled people. Website: www.spuc.org.uk.

If laughter is the best medicine, the following have been found to possess healing qualities (the list is not exhaustive, but might prove exhausting): Jerome K. Jerome's *Three Men in a Boat*; P. G. Wodehouse's Jeeves and Wooster stories; Charles Dickens' *The Pickwick Papers*; Richmal Crompton's *Just William* stories; the essays of G. K. Chesterton.

PRAYERS AND DEVOTIONS

Prayer is strength for the weak. (John Paul II)

On his historic visit to Britain in 1982 Pope John Paul II implored us not to drive the vulnerable to the margins of society. The Church needs to set an example of inclusiveness for disabled people by improving access, accommodation and facilities, such as installing hearing loops (and ensuring that they function!) However, although physical participation in the life of the Church is preferable, sometimes it is not possible. In this case, arrangements can be made for the sick and housebound to hear confession, and for the Eucharist to be brought to the home. This brings great comfort to the individual, but the individual can also join spiritually with the Church. We can unite in prayer with our parish at Mass-time; it is also possible to watch a Mass on the EWTN TV channel. We can unite with other Catholics in adoration of the Blessed Sacrament, perhaps using a picture as an aid. The home itself can be blessed, and a 'sacred space' can help us focus on God, with a blessed crucifix and images set apart from domestic bustle. This helps us not just to talk to God but to listen, and can also act as a visible and tangible reminder of our discipleship.

PRAYERS

The Sign of the Cross

In the name of the Father
And of the Son
And of the Holy Spirit.

The Lord's Prayer

Our Father who art in heaven,
Hallowed be thy name.
Thy kingdom come.
Thy will be done on earth, as it is in heaven.
Give us this day our daily bread,
And forgive us our trespasses,
As we forgive those who trespass against us;
And lead us not into temptation,
But deliver us from evil.
Amen.

Hail Mary[1]

Hail Mary, full of grace, the Lord is with thee.
Blessed art thou among women
And blessed is the fruit of thy womb, Jesus.
Holy Mary, Mother of God,
Pray for us sinners,
Now and at the hour of our death.
Amen.

To The Guardian Angel

O angel of God, my guardian dear,
To whom God's love commits me here,
Ever this day be at my side,
To light and guard,
To rule and guide. Amen

Prayer in Honour of the Five Wounds

Act of Contrition

As I kneel before Thee on the Cross, most loving Saviour of my soul, my conscience reproaches me with having nailed Thee to that Cross with these hands of mine, as often as I have fallen into mortal sin, wearying Thee with my base ingratitude. My God, my chief and perfect good, worthy of all my love, because Thou hast loaded me with blessings; I cannot now undo my misdeeds, as I would most willingly; but I loathe them, grieving sincerely for having offended Thee, Who art infinite goodness. And now, kneeling at Thy feet, I try, at least, to compassionate Thee, to give Thee thanks, to ask Thee pardon and contrition; wherefore with my heart and lips, I say:

To the Wound of the Left Foot

Holy Wound of the left foot of my Jesus, I adore Thee; I compassionate Thee, O Jesus, for the most bitter pain which Thou didst suffer. I thank Thee for the love whereby Thou laboured to overtake me on the way to ruin, and didst bleed amid the thorns and brambles of my sins. I offer to the Eternal Father the pain and love of Thy most holy humanity, in atonement for my sins, all of which I detest with sincere and bitter contrition. (Recite one Our Father, one Hail Mary, and one Glory Be.)

Holy Mother, pierce me through,
In my heart each wound renew
Of my Saviour crucified.

To the Wound of the Right Foot

Holy wound of the right foot of my Jesus, I adore Thee; I compassionate Thee, O Jesus, for the most bitter pain which Thou didst suffer. I thank Thee for that love which pierced Thee with such torture and shedding of blood, in order to punish my wanderings and the guilty pleasures I have granted to my unbridled passions. I offer the Eternal Father all the pain and love of Thy most holy humanity, and I pray Thee for grace to weep over my sins with hot tears, and to enable me to persevere in the good which I have begun, without ever swerving again from my obedience to the divine commands.
(Recite one Our Father, one Hail Mary, and one Glory Be.)

Holy Mother, pierce me through,
In my heart each wound renew
Of my Saviour crucified.

To the Wound of the Left Hand

Holy Wound of the left hand of my Jesus, I adore Thee; I compassionate Thee, O Jesus, for the most bitter pain which Thou didst suffer. I thank Thee for having in Thy love spared me the scourges and eternal damnation which my sins have merited. I offer to the Eternal Father the pain and love of Thy most holy humanity, and I pray Thee to teach me how to turn to good account my span of life, and bring forth in it worthy fruits of penance, and to disarm the justice of God, which I have provoked.
(Recite one Our Father, one Hail Mary, and one Glory Be.)

Holy Mother, pierce me through,
In my heart each wound renew
Of my Saviour crucified.

To the Wound of the Right Hand

Holy Wound of the right hand of my Jesus, I adore Thee; I compassionate Thee, O Jesus, for the most bitter pain which Thou didst suffer. I thank Thee for Thy graces lavished on me with such love, in spite of all my most perverse obstinacy. I offer to the Eternal Father all the pain and love of Thy most holy humanity, and I pray Thee to change my heart and its affections, and make me do all my actions in accordance with the will of God.
(Recite one Our Father, one Hail Mary, and one Glory Be.)

Holy Mother, pierce me through,
In my heart each wound renew
Of my Saviour crucified.

To the Wound of the Sacred Side

Holy Wound in the side of my Jesus, I adore Thee; I compassionate Thee, O Jesus, for the cruel insult Thou didst suffer. I thank Thee, my Jesus, for the love which suffered Thy side and Heart to be pierced, so that the last drops of blood and water might issue forth, making my redemption to overflow. I offer to the Eternal Father this outrage, and the love of Thy most holy humanity, that my soul may enter once for all into that most loving Heart, eager and ready to receive the greatest sinners, and never more depart.
(Recite one Our Father, one Hail Mary, and one Glory Be.)

Holy Mother, pierce me through,
In my heart each wound renew
Of my Saviour crucified.

Chaplet of the Five Wounds

This Passionist chaplet was devised by Father Paul Aloysius, sixth superior general of the Passionists. The devotion also honours the mystery of the risen Christ, with the marks of the Five Wounds. Pope Leo XII approved the chaplet on 11 August 1823; it was approved again in 1851. Each of the five divisions is composed of five Glories in honour of Christ's Wounds and one Ave in commemoration of the Sorrowful Mother. The chaplet must be blessed by the Passionist superior or a delegation from him.

Format of the chaplet

The chaplet has 25 beads, grouped into five sets. Each of the five mysteries is associated with a scriptural meditation:

- Jesus is conceived by the Holy Spirit and the Virgin Mary
- The Spirit of the Lord rests on Jesus
- Jesus is led by the Holy Spirit into the desert
- The Holy Spirit in the Church
- The Holy Spirit in the souls of the faithful.

Rosary of the Five Wounds

The Rosary of the Holy Wounds was introduced at the beginning of the twentieth century by the Venerable Sister Mary Martha Chambon, a lay Roman Catholic Sister of the Monastery of the Visitation Order in Chambéry, France, who was instructed to revive the Holy Wounds devotion. Part of this devotion can be a Chaplet of Mercy of the Holy Wounds of Jesus, based on her private revelations. The chaplet was approved for the Institute of Visitation in 1912, and extended to all the faithful by the Sacred Penitentiary in 1924. The Rosary of the Holy Wounds, revealed to Chambon, is prayed on a standard five decade rosary.

Format of the rosary

This consists of prayers said on specific portions of the rosary beads:

Prayers on the Crucifix and first three beads:

Bead one: O Jesus, Divine Redeemer, be merciful to us and to the whole world. Amen.
Bead two: Strong God, Holy God, Immortal God, have mercy on us and on the whole world. Amen
Bead three: Grace and Mercy, O my Jesus, during present dangers; cover us with Your Precious Blood. Amen.
Finish with this invocation:
Eternal Father, grant us mercy through the Blood of Jesus Christ, Your only Son; grant us mercy we beseech You. Amen, Amen, Amen.

This prayer is said on the large beads (Our Father Beads):

Eternal Father, I offer You the Wounds of Our Lord, Jesus Christ, to heal the wounds of our souls.

This prayer is said on the small beads (Hail Mary beads):

My Jesus, pardon and mercy, through the merits of Your Holy Wounds.

Litany to the Sacred Head of Jesus[2]

Lord have mercy on us	Lord have mercy on us
Christ have mercy on us	Christ have mercy on us
Lord have mercy on us	Lord have mercy on us
Christ hear us	Christ graciously hear us

God the Father of Heaven, have mercy on us.

God the Son, Redeemer of the World, have mercy on us.

God the Holy Ghost, have mercy on us.

Sacred Head of Jesus, formed by the Holy Ghost in the womb of the Virgin Mary, guide us in all our ways;

Sacred Head of Jesus, substantially united to the Word of God, guide us in all our ways; Sacred Head of Jesus, Temple of Divine Wisdom, guide us in all our ways;

Sacred Head of Jesus, Centre of Eternal Light, guide us in all our ways;

Sacred Head of Jesus, Tabernacle of Divine Knowledge, guide us in all our ways;

Sacred Head of Jesus, Safeguard against Error, guide us in all our ways;

Sacred Head of Jesus, Sunshine of Heaven and Earth, guide us in all our ways;

Sacred Head of Jesus, Treasure of Science and Pledge of Faith, guide us in all our ways;

Sacred Head of Jesus, Radiant with Beauty and Justice and Love, guide us in all our ways; Sacred Head of Jesus, full of Grace and Truth, guide us in all our ways;

Sacred Head of Jesus, Living Witness of Humility, guide us in all our ways;

Sacred Head of Jesus, reflecting the Infinite Majesty of God, guide us in all our ways;

Sacred Head of Jesus, Centre of the Universe, guide us in all our ways;

Sacred Head of Jesus, object of the Father's Joyous Satisfaction, guide us in all our ways;

Sacred Head of Jesus, upon which the Holy Ghost rested, guide us in all our ways;

Sacred Head of Jesus, around which the Glory of Mount Tabor Shone, guide us in all our ways;

Sacred Head of Jesus, Who had no place on Earth on which to rest, guide us in all our ways;

Sacred Head of Jesus, Whom the fragrant anointing of Magdalen consoled, guide us in all our ways;

Sacred Head of Jesus, bathed with the Sweat of Blood in Gethsemane, guide us in all our ways;

Sacred Head of Jesus, Who wept for our sins, guide us in all our ways;

Sacred Head of Jesus, crowned with Thorns, guide us in all our ways;

Sacred Head of Jesus, outraged by the indignities of the Passion, guide us in all our ways;

Sacred Head of Jesus, consoled by the loving gesture of Veronica, guide us in all our ways;

Sacred Head of Jesus, bowed to Earth which was Redeemed at the moment of death on the Calvary, guide us in all our ways;

Sacred Head of Jesus, Light of every being born on Earth, guide us in all our ways;

Sacred Head of Jesus, our Guide and our Hope, guide us in all our ways;

Sacred Head of Jesus, Who knows all our needs, guide us in all our ways;

Sacred Head of Jesus, Who gives us all Graces, guide us in all our ways;

Sacred Head of Jesus, that governs all the motions of the Sacred Heart, guide us in all our ways;

Sacred Head of Jesus, Whom we wish to adore and make known throughout the World, guide us in all our ways;

Sacred Head of Jesus, Who knows all the secrets of our hearts, guide us in all our ways;

Sacred Head of Jesus, Who enraptures Angels and the Saints, guide us in all our ways;

Sacred Head of Jesus, Whom one day we hope to behold unveiled forever, guide us in all our ways;

Jesus, we adore Your Sacred Head; we surrender utterly to all the Decrees of Your infinite Wisdom.

Prayers to Mary, our Mother of Mercy especially for the sick

(Feast of our Lady of Lourdes, 11 February)

O Mother of Mercy,
health of the sick, refuge of sinners, comfort of the afflicted,
you know our wants, our troubles, our sufferings;
please listen to our prayers today
for all those who are sick and especially those who have asked for our prayers
and those for whom we have promised to pray *(names)*.
We come to you with unbounded confidence, as children to their Mother,
to ask you to speak with us and for us to your Son,
our Lord Jesus Christ, that He may make those for whom we pray better physically and spiritually.
We ask this through Christ our Lord.
Amen

> *O Mary, conceived without sin, pray for us who have recourse to thee.*

Litany of Our Lady of Lourdes[3]

Lord have mercy. Christ have mercy. Lord have mercy.

Christ hear us. Christ graciously hear us.

God the Father of Heaven, have mercy on us.

God the Son, Redeemer of the world, have mercy on us.

God the Holy Spirit, have mercy on us.

Holy Trinity, one God, have mercy on us.

Holy Mary, pray for us.

Holy Mother of God, pray for us.

Mother of Christ, pray for us.

Mother of our Saviour, pray for us.

Our Lady of Lourdes, help of Christians, pray for us.

Our Lady of Lourdes, source of love, pray for us.

Our Lady of Lourdes, mother of the poor, pray for us.

Our Lady of Lourdes, mother of the handicapped, pray for us.

Our Lady of Lourdes, mother of orphans, pray for us.

Our Lady of Lourdes, mother of all children, pray for us.

Our Lady of Lourdes, mother of all nations, pray for us.

Our Lady of Lourdes, mother of the Church, pray for us.

Our Lady of Lourdes, friend of the lonely, pray for us.

Our Lady of Lourdes, comforter of those who mourn, pray for us.

Our Lady of Lourdes, shelter of the homeless, pray for us.

Our Lady of Lourdes, guide of travellers, pray for us.

Our Lady of Lourdes, strength of the weak, pray for us.

Our Lady of Lourdes, refuge of sinners, pray for us.

Our Lady of Lourdes, comforter of the suffering, pray for us.

Our Lady of Lourdes, help of the dying, pray for us.

Queen of Heaven, pray for us.

Queen of peace, pray for us.

Lamb of God, you take away the sins of the world, spare us O Lord.

Lamb of God, you take away the sins of the world, graciously hear us, O Lord.

Lamb of God, you take away the sins of the world, have mercy on us.

Christ hear us, Christ graciously hear us.

Let us pray:

Grant us, your servants, we pray you, Lord God,
to enjoy perpetual health of mind and body.

By the glorious intercession of Blessed Mary ever Virgin,
may we be delivered from present sorrows,
and enjoy everlasting happiness.
We ask this through Christ our Lord. Amen.

Memorare

Remember, O most gracious Virgin Mary,
That never was it known
That anyone who fled to your protection,
Implored your help, Or sought your intercession
Was left unaided.
Inspired with this confidence,
I fly to you, O Virgin of virgins, My Mother.
To you I come, Before you I stand, Sinful and sorrowful.
Despise not my prayers and petitions,
But in your mercy, hear and answer me.
Amen.

Salve Regina

Hail, Holy Queen, Mother of Mercy!
Hail, our life, our sweetness,
And our hope!
To you do we cry, poor banished children of Eve!
To you do we send up our sighs,
Mourning and weeping in this valley of tears!
Turn then, most gracious advocate,
Your eyes of mercy toward us,
And after this our exile,
Show unto us the Blessed Fruit of your womb, Jesus!
O clement, O loving, O sweet Virgin Mary!
Pray for us, O holy Mother of God,
That we may be made worthy
Of the promises of Christ.

Stabat Mater Dolorosa
('The Sorrowful Mother Stood')

At the Cross

Her station keeping,

Stood the Mournful Mother weeping,

Close to Jesus at the last.

Through her heart, his sorrow sharing,

All his bitter anguish bearing,

Now at length the sword had passed.

Oh, how sad and sore distressed

Was that Mother highly blest

Of the sole-begotten One!

O dear Mother, fount of love,

Touch my spirit from above;

Make my heart with yours accord.

Make me feel as you have felt;

Make my heart to glow and melt

With the love of Christ my Lord.

Glory Be

Glory be to the Father,
and to the Son, and to the Holy Spirit.
As it was in the beginning, is now,
And ever shall be, world without end.
Amen.

The Apostles' Creed

I believe in God
The Father almighty,
Creator of heaven and earth.
I believe in Jesus Christ,
His only Son, our Lord.

He was conceived by the power of the Holy Spirit
And born of the Virgin Mary.
He suffered under Pontius Pilate,
Was crucified, died, and was buried.
He descended to the dead.
On the third day he rose again.
He ascended into heaven
And is seated at the right hand of the Father.
He will come again to judge the living and the dead.
I believe in the Holy Spirit,
The holy catholic Church,
The communion of saints,
The forgiveness of sins,
The resurrection of the body,
And life everlasting.
Amen.

Prayer to St Michael

St Michael, Archangel, defend us in battle.
Be our protection against the malice and snares of the Devil.
May God rebuke him, we humbly pray.
And do you, O Prince of the heavenly host,
By the Divine power,
Thrust into Hell Satan and all the evil spirits
Who prowl about the world,
Seeking the ruin of souls.
Amen.

Act of Contrition

O my God, I am heartily sorry for having offended Thee,
And I detest all my sins,
Because I dread the loss of Heaven and the pains of Hell,
But most of all because they offend Thee, my God,
Who art all-good and deserving of all my love.
I firmly resolve, with the help of Thy grace to confess my sins,
To do penance,

And to amend my life.
Amen.

Prayer of Contrition

O my God, because you are so good,
I am very sorry that I have sinned against you,
And with the help of your good grace,
I will not sin again.
Through Jesus Christ Our Lord.
Amen.

Prayer for Healing[4]

Lord Jesus, through the love of the Father
And the power of the Holy Spirit
Fill my life with the gift of healing.
Remove from me any fear
That blocks my awareness
Of your caring presence.
Reach into my heart
And heal any hurt that has broken it.
Every pain that I have caused to another heart...
Heal that as well.
Any relationship in my life that has been damaged...
Heal those relationships.
Give me the courage to be
An instrument of your peace.
Radiate my spirit with healing
For all spiritual cancers –
Criticism, complaint, and control.
Heal me of anything
That would keep others from seeing your presence in my life.
Touch me Jesus in mind, body and spirit,
In all the ways I need it the most.
If it is God's will for me,
Grant the physical and emotional healings I seek.
But most of all, grant me a loving heart

And the resolve to accept
The answers you give to my prayer,
Knowing that you are always faithful to the promise...
That in all things God works for the good
Of those who love Him.

A Morning Prayer

Dear Father, Give to me this day
The light of Christ to show the way,
The love of Christ, to help me see
All in Christ's light, and perfectly
The way of Christ; and so this day,
To see the Christ who is the Way.
Amen.

Night prayers

Dear Father, Give to me this night
The comfort of Christ's holy light;
The courage of His Spirit's breath
To keep my soul from fear of death;
And in the Father's holy might
Sleep gently, gently through the night.
Amen.

Dear Father, Take my pain this night
To help the helpless in their plight;
To save the hopeless from all care,
And save my soul from chill despair.
And so, good Father, hear us call;
Bring good from evil for us all.
Amen.

A Litany of the Eucharist

Body of Christ, find me.

Body of Christ, hide me.

Body of Christ, help me.
Body of Christ, keep me.
Body of Christ, surround me.
Body of Christ, sustain me.
Body of Christ, strengthen me.
Body of Christ, sanctify me.
Body of Christ, save me.
Body of Christ, love me.
Body of Christ, hold me.
Body of Christ, heal me.

The Rosary

The Rosary usually begins with the Apostles' Creed, said while holding the crucifix of the Rosary. The Our Father is said on the first lone bead, then three Hail Marys on the next three small beads, followed by a Glory Be. A Hail Mary is said on each small bead on the main string of the Rosary, in five groups of ten (called 'decades'), each concluding with a Glory Be, with an Our Father on the large beads in between. The Rosary helps us meditate on the 'mysteries' in the life of Jesus and his Mother—the Joyful, Luminous, Sorrowful and Glorious Mysteries—totalling twenty. The Joyful Mysteries concern the conception, birth and childhood of Our Lord; the Luminous Mysteries focus on the public ministry of Jesus Christ; the Sorrowful Mysteries concern his suffering and death; the Glorious Mysteries concern Our Lord's Resurrection and the celestial mysteries thereafter.[5]

The Divine Mercy

The Divine Mercy cycle of prayers originated with the Polish mystic St Faustina, and is recited on rosary beads, beginning with the Our Father, the Hail Mary and the Creed on the three large beads. On each decade, say:
For the sake of His sorrowful Passion have mercy on us and on the whole world.

On each large bead, say:
Eternal Father, I offer you the Body and Blood, Soul and Divinity of your dearly beloved Son, Our Lord Jesus Christ in atonement for our sins and those of the whole world.

Conclude with:
Holy God, Holy Mighty One, Holy Immortal One, have mercy on us and on the whole world. (*Three times.*)

Novenas

Novenas are cycles of prayers, said over nine days, modelled on the prayers said by the Disciples and Our Lady after the Ascension of Jesus, as they waited nine days for the coming of the Holy Spirit. They are directed to the Saints, especially St Jude, St Rita, St Antony and St Anne, for special intentions. Detailed instructions can be found in prayer books.

Notes

[1] The Hail Mary consists of the Angel Gabriel's greeting to Our Lady at the Annunciation (Luke 1:26–31) and a request for her to pray for us.
[2] From C. Kerr, *Teresa Helena Higginson*, with an Introduction by P. Haffner (Leominster: Gracewing, 2008), p. 373.

3 From *Mercy Associates Prayer Book*, available at: http://www.merciful.org/prayerbook/our-ladyoflourdes.html.
4 Prayer from *His Love Ministries*, Rev. John F. Campoli, I.V. Dei, available at: www.hisloveministries.com.
5 Detailed instructions on how to pray the rosary can be found in prayer books, or on websites like www.rosary-center.org. Pope John Paul II in his Apostolic Letter *Rosarium Virginis Mariae* introduced the Luminous Mysteries in October 2002.

www.ingramcontent.com/pod-product-compliance
Lightning Source LLC
Chambersburg PA
CBHW020009050426
42450CB00005B/386